The Public's Right to Know

Timely Reports to Keep
Journalists, Scholars and the Public
Abreast of Developing Issues, Events and Trends

Published by Congressional Quarterly Inc.
1414 22nd Street, N.W.
Washington, D.C. 20037

60679

About the Cover

The cover was designed by Art Director Richard Pottern.

PRINTED IN THE UNITED STATES OF AMERICA
August 1980

Editor, Hoyt Gimlin
Associate Editor, Sandra Stencel
Editorial Assistants, Karen Rohan, Claire Tury
Production Manager, I. D. Fuller
Assistant Production Manager, Maceo Mayo

Libary of Congress Cataloging in Publication Data
Main entry under title:

Editorial research reports on the public's right to know.

Bibliography: p.
Includes index.
1. Freedom of information — United States. 2. Privacy, Right of — United States. I. Congressional Quarterly, inc. II. Title: The public's right to know.
JC599.U5E34   · 323.44'5'0973   80-20610 ·
ISBN 0-87187-157-2 ·

Contents

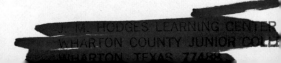

Foreword

"The Public's Right to Know," this book's title, is closer to being a question than it is a statement. The phrase has a First Amendment ring, readily invoked in arguments on behalf of freedom of speech and press. But since the birth of the Constitution, there has been no agreement on just how much the public is entitled to know in countless situations, especially matters affecting national security or, more recently, personal privacy.

Some of the conflicts are rooted in the Constitution itself, such as when the freedom-of-press provision clashes with the Sixth Amendment's fair-trial guarantee. The historic adversary relationship between the press and the judiciary, with some new twists, is recounted in "The Supreme Court and the Press," one of the nine related Reports that make up this book. All have previously been published individually by Editorial Research Reports.

Citizens who want an open society but still a secure nation are vexed by the dilemma outlined in the Report on "Atomic Security." The basic question, "When does a paternalistic government know best?," recurs also in the Reports on "Determining Radiation Dangers" and "Assassinations Inquiry." And the value placed on individual privacy must be balanced against such public needs are outlined in the Reports on "Census Taking" and "Freedom of Information Act: A Reappraisal."

Many of the privacy-vs.-public benefit issues arise out of today's technology. Computers make information more available, for ultimate good or bad, as "America's Information Boom" Report portrays. And "Television in the Eighties" tells how a combination of new electronics and a gradual deregulation of the nation's airwaves are bringing a flood of information and entertainment into American homes. No one currently can foresee all of the potential benefits or consequences.

Hoyt Gimlin
Editor

Washington, D.C.
August 1980

TELEVISION IN THE EIGHTIES

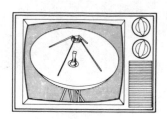

by

Marc Leepson

**May 9
1980**

(**Report update:** Cable News Network, mentioned on page 9, began broadcasting on June 1, 1980, as scheduled.)

TELEVISION IN THE EIGHTIES

A FTER nearly four decades of commercial television broadcasting, the medium employs space-age satellites and computer technology to provide nearly 76 million American households[1] with instantaneous presentations of news, sports and entertainment *(See box, p. 10)*. Yet, technologically speaking, television is still in its infancy. A combination of new advances in home video electronics, satellite-transmitted cable television, information retrieval systems and a deregulatory climate in Washington are certain to alter the content of television radically in the coming decade.

Typical of prophecies of things to come, Desmond Smith of the Canadian Broadcasting Corp. writes that "the kind of storm that swept Dorothy off to Oz is about to hit the old broadcasting industry, and the American public — which owns the public airways — is likely to be the beneficiary."[2] The most visible change will be a much wider choice of programs for television viewers. Today most TV sets can tune in no more than seven very high frequency (VHF) stations and a smattering of others in the ultra high frequency (UHF) range. But the 16 million American households that receive cable television now can view up to 36 channels. The technology is in place to increase that number to 54 in the near future.

Cable television has the potential to deliver up to 80 channels to each subscriber. Filling these channels are the rapidly growing cable and pay-cable television industries, subscription television stations and so-called "superstations" *(see Glossary)*. More than one observer has noted that the future of television will consist of a change from broadcasting to "narrowcasting" — featuring a wide choice of televised offerings, each tailored for narrow sections of the viewing public.

From its beginning, nationwide commercial television has been dominated by the major networks.[3] But the networks are facing direct competition for the first time as more and more

---

[1] The figure is based on a current estimate by Arbitron, the television rating service, that 75,793,500 American households are equipped with television sets.

[2] Writing in *The New York Times Magazine,* Aug. 19, 1979, p. 16.

[3] American Broadcasting Co. (ABC), Columbia Broadcasting System (CBS) and National Broadcasting Co. (NBC), the three major commercial networks, provide programming for affiliated stations and those they own and operate. Public Broadcasting System (PBS), a major network, often provides programs that are underwritten by corporate funding but it is not a commercial network in the sense that ABC, CBS and NBC are.

Americans choose to augment their standard television fare with home video equipment and services like pay-cable and subscription television. Network executives have expressed concern that these increasingly popular modes will take viewers away from local network affiliates and that advertisers will look elsewhere. Others say the networks' fears are akin to those of the motion picture makers when commercial television arrived; the movie moguls thought it would drive them out of business. Some film studios have suffered setbacks, but it can be argued that television actually has helped the motion picture industry. For one thing, the movie companies now produce most of the network television shows. In addition, the studios have made millions of dollars selling television rights to the networks.

FCC's Move Toward Cable Deregulation

The federal government, through the Federal Communications Commission (FCC), has until recently been a major factor in the networks' domination of the television airwaves. The Communications Act of 1934 required the agency to "provide a fair, efficient and equitable distribution" of broadcasting facilities across the nation. In accordance with that provision, the commission in 1952 promulgated a basic plan for nationwide allocation of available television channels. An early priority was to assign each community at least one television station. This had the effect of protecting local television stations from competition, including competition from cable television systems.[4]

The FCC prohibited cable construction in large television markets, and limited the types of programs cable operators could show and the number of channels they could offer subscribers. But beginning in 1970, the agency softened its opposition and, one by one, eliminated most of the restrictions on cable television. This deregulation of television accelerated three years ago when Charles D. Ferris, a lawyer and ex-aide to former Senate Majority Leader Mike Mansfield, was appointed FCC chairman.

Ferris

Ferris recently explained the commission's deregulation philosophy as it applies to television broadcasting. "I think our role is to have no bias toward any of the methods by which the American public receives its

---

[4] See "Community Antenna TV," *E.R.R.*, 1964 Vol. II, pp. 921-940.

> ## Television Glossary
>
> **Cable television.** Originally used solely to help households pick up weak television signals, its uses have broadened and today reach 16 million subscribers who pay for the service.
>
> **Pay-cable.** It provides cable subscribers, at extra cost, with commercial-free programming, including movies and special events.
>
> **Subscription television (STV).** A range of programs are transmitted via satellite directly into the home where a decoder is used, for a fee, to bring them into focus.
>
> **Superstation.** An independent local station that beams its signals to a satellite which relays them to local cable systems across the country. Four such stations are now in operation.

programming," Ferris said. "The over-the-air broadcasters have many competitors for delivery of video programming. All of these alternative methods of bringing either live events or entertainment programs to viewers to a great extent should be done by marketplace forces from the standpoint of who can provide the most to the viewers. The choice should be made by viewers rather than by intermediaries — whether the intermediary is the government or the corporate structure. I think the more potential the viewers have to make these choices, the better."[5]

Rapid Growth of Cable and 'Pay-Cable'

The FCC's move toward television broadcasting deregulation has benefited the cable and pay-cable television industries most. Moreover, both media have experienced significant technological breakthroughs in the last five years, notably in satellite transmission capability. Cable television dates from 1949 when a powerful television antenna was erected atop a 50-foot mast on a hill near Astoria, Ore., to help 11 households pick up weak television signals from Seattle.[6] The first community antenna television (CATV or cable) company was founded in 1950 in Lansford, Pa., by Robert J. Tarlton, the owner of a radio and television repair shop. Tarlton's Panther Valley Television built a master antenna atop a mountain that was blocking the reception of television signals from Philadelphia, 65 miles away. The signals were amplified and then fed into a cable strung on poles down the mountain and into the town. Panther Valley Television charged its users an installation fee of $125 and a monthly service fee of $3.

During cable television's first 25 years the service was used primarily for rural residents to receive faraway television signals. By 1959, there were 560 operating cable systems with 550,000 subscribers. A modest growth continued until 1978, when deregulation gave it a spurt. The cable industry expanded

---

[5] Interview, April 4, 1980.
[6] See "Cable Television: The Coming Medium," *E.R.R.*, 1970 Vol. II, pp. 667-686, and Mary Alice Mayer Phillips, *CATV: A History of Community Antenna Televison* (1972).

The Cable Business

Cable television is a big business, and by law only one cable system may operate in a community. Determining which cable system wins the exclusive franchise for a community often is bitterly contested by cable entrepreneurs. Local governments have the franchise-granting power. In small and medium-size cities, especially, the process can be tinged with unpleasant political bargaining.

Twelve of the nation's top 30 television markets have cable systems in operation, serving at least part of their total broadcast areas, a recent *Broadcasting* magazine survey found. Most of the areas which have not chosen a cable system are considering doing so and have attracted many interested investors. In Philadelphia, 10 firms have bid for the city's cable franchise. In suburban Fairfax County, Va., near Washington, D.C., 19 companies have expressed interest.

Competition for cable licenses has led to numerous lawsuits and legal actions involving irregularities in the franchising process. One cable operator, Irving Kahn, former chairman of Teleprompter, was convicted in 1973 of bribing officials in Johnstown, Pa. Five years from now there should be no more competitive maneuvering to win cable licenses. By that time all the cable franchises in the country are expected to be allocated.

by 25 percent that year and 20 percent the next year. According to the National Cable Television Association, 4,100 cable systems serve 16 million subscribers. Cable television is seen in every state and accounts for one-fifth of the nation's households that receive television. This boom shows no let-up. During the past two decades, some 200,000 miles of cable lines were laid; in 1980 alone, *Business Week* magazine reports, the 50 leading cable companies expect to string 43,000 miles.[7]

Cable television's recent growth has also been stimulated by "pay cable." It began in 1975 when Home Box Office (HBO), owned by Time-Life Inc., began making uncut, commercial-free movies and top-flight entertainment programs available to local cable systems. HBO is beamed nationwide via the RCA-owned Satcom I satellite which was launched in 1975 *(see p. 18).* Pay cable systems like HBO now serve nearly 5.8 million subscribers, according to *CableVision* magazine.

Cable subscribers, who pay a basic monthly fee of about $7.50, have the option of paying an additonal $8 to $10 a month for a pay system such as HBO. A cable system's main expense in delivering pay cable to its subscribers is buying and installing a satellite receiving station. Home Box Office, with more than four million subscribers, is the leader in the field. Its competitors include Showtime, Front Row, Take 5 and The Movie Channel.

[7] *Business Week*, Dec. 17, 1979, pp. 60-66.

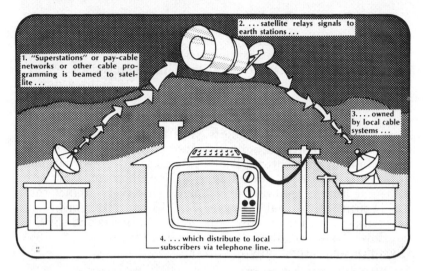

1. "Superstations" or pay-cable networks or other cable programming is beamed to satellite...

2. ...satellite relays signals to earth stations...

3. ...owned by local cable systems...

4. ...which distribute to local subscribers via telephone line.

The Getty Oil Co. and four large Hollywood motion picture studios recently announced plans to form a new pay-cable operation. Columbia Pictures, MCA, Paramount, Twentieth Century-Fox and Getty will begin their as-yet-unnamed venture early next year. The studios announced April 22 that they will give the network exclusive rights to all of their new movies for nine months once they are made available to pay-cable. This arrangement, *Broadcasting* magazine commented, "sent shockwaves throughout the pay-cable world" because it "would effectively prohibit ... the other national pay-cable services from exhibiting the films of those four studios within the time frames generally considered acceptable to the pay-cable industry. Approximately 60 percent of HBO's movie schedule comes from the four companies."[8]

Aside from pay-cable, cable systems now are able to offer other satellite-relayed channels at no additional cost to subscribers. These channels, which have commercials, include the Christian Broadcasting Network, featuring religious programming; the Cable Satellite Public Affairs Network, offering continuous coverage of the U.S. House of Representatives when it is in session; Galavision, a Spanish-language channel; Cineamerica, whose programming is directed at persons over age 50; Black Entertainment Television; and a host of 24-hour-a-day "data" channels offering news headlines, stock prices, weather reports and similar information.

Sports events are popular cable attractions. The Madison Square Garden Sports Network carries more than 350 sports events a year and is seen by five million cable subscribers nationwide. The Entertainment and Sports Programming Network (ESPN) is beamed into four million homes across the

---

[8] *Broadcasting,* April 28, 1980, p. 22.

country by some 600 cable systems. ESPN, which began broadcasting last Sept. 7, runs continuously from 6 p.m. Friday until early Monday morning and for at least 15 hours each weekday. By early next year, it plans to be on the air 24 hours a day.

ESPN has hired experienced network sports announcers and executives; its chief operating officer is Chester R. Simmons, former president of NBC Sports. The Getty Oil Co. owns 85 percent of the sports network and reportedly has invested some $10 million in the venture. The network has attracted national advertising contracts, including a $1.3 million account with Anheuser-Busch, the brewery company. Observers predict that ESPN soon will be challenging ABC, CBS and NBC for broadcast rights to such major events as the World Series and the Super Bowl. Last year, its bid for the right to broadcast the 1984 Olympics was second only to ABC's.

Satellite-Aided Local TV 'Superstations'

Another feature of cable television is the "superstation," a single independent television station that beams its signal to an earth-orbiting satellite which relays it to local cable systems across the country. There are four such stations in operation: WTBS (formerly WTCG) in Atlanta, WOR in New York, WGN in Chicago and KTVU in San Francisco. The pioneer superstation is Atlanta's WTBS, owned by R.E. "Ted" Turner III, the 41-year-old advertising millionaire and sportsman.[9]

The idea of a superstation originated with Turner after the FCC in 1974, under a new "open skies" policy, overturned a ruling that severely limited the number of companies that could operate and use broadcast satellites. One result was that cable systems nationwide could pick up signals by satellite without permission from the broadcaster of the signal and without paying for the signal they received. The major advantage to the superstation is that it can sell advertising for national rates. In addition, it receives up to 10 cents per subscriber from the local cable systems.

Turner

Turner began distributing the WTBS signal nationwide at the end of 1976. WTBS now reaches some 7.2 million homes through 1,710 cable systems in 48 states

---

[9] Turner owns the Atlanta Braves professional baseball team and the Atlanta Hawks pro basketball team. He gained further fame when he skippered his 12-meter sailing yacht *Courageous* to victory in the 1978 America's Cup race.

— all but Alaska and Hawaii. Its fare consists largely of baseball, basketball, old movies, television reruns, children's programs and second-run series produced by the British Broadcasting Corp.

Turner's newest broadcasting venture is the Cable News Network (CNN), which is scheduled to be beamed to three or four million cable subscribers nationwide, beginning June 1. CNN will be the nation's first 24-hour all-news television station. Turner reportedly has invested at least $30 million in it thus far. He is reported to have committed $20 million a year to the network for its first five years. He has hired a number of former network journalists and executives. News commentary will also be provided by ex-Congresswoman Bella Abzug, anti-feminist Phyllis Schlafly, former Treasury Secretary William Simon, psychologist Joyce Brothers, financial writer Dan Dorfman and Washington columnists Roland Evans and Robert Novak. Daniel Schorr, formerly of CBS, will be the cable network's chief correspondent.

Industry observers say that to break even CNN will need to reach 7.5 million cable subscribers and win large advertising contracts. Turner predicts that within five years his programming will be viewed in half of the homes in the country. Others are not sure CNN will be that successful. They point out that its $20 million a year budget does not measure up to the networks' spending on news — and they devote only a few hours of broadcast time each day to news. There is a chance, moreover, that CNN will not be able to use the space it had reserved on Satcom I. CNN's application has been challenged by the Spanish International Network, and the legal maneuvering could delay the network's scheduled opening on June 1.

Subscription TV; Two-Way Experiments

Another dimension of the pay-cable system is subscription television (STV), which, in fact, is not delivered via cable. STV, in existence only since 1977, is transmitted to the home TV set by satellite. Its main advantage over cable is that it requires no wires. The cost of stringing wires may run as much as $100,000 a mile in older cities.

An STV subscriber pays about $25 for a small decoding device to unscramble as many as 20 channels of satellite-sent signals. In addition, the subscriber pays about $17 a month for the service which, like cable, includes programming from local and faraway commercial stations. And like pay-cable, it includes commercial-free movies and entertainment. STV currently is in operation only in Los Angeles, New York, Boston, Detroit and Phoenix, but industry analysts say it may be seen in 20 cities by the end of the year.

Origins of Commercial Television

No precise agreed-upon date fixes the beginning of television broadcasting. During the 1930s and 1940s several stations experimented with television. For millions of Americans, their first glimpse of the new marvel called television came at the 1939 New York World's Fair, where demonstration sets were on view.

The Federal Communications Commission authorized the start of commercial television broadcasting on July 1, 1941, and 10 stations were on the air by the following May, reaching minuscule audiences. By this time, America was in World War II and the nation's wartime electronic needs arrested television's development.

By 1948, three years after the end of the war, 20 commercial stations were on the air. From that time forward, the number grew rapidly — and so did the nation's TV audience. Today 746 commercial (both VHF and UHF) and 267 public ("educational") television stations operate in the United states.

The Los Angeles STV station, National Subscription Television, went into operation in April 1977, and now has more than 225,000 subscribers. The New York City metropolitan area's STV station, WWHT-TV in West Orange, N.J., has 65,000 customers. The whole industry was aided by a 1979 FCC ruling which overturned a regulation that limited STV stations to one per community.

A technologically advanced form of subscription television was proposed last August by Communications Satellite Corp. (Comsat), the leading manufacturer of satellites used for television and telephone connections. As envisioned by Comsat's satellite-to-home subscription system, there would be available to viewers by 1983 a $200 rooftop dish antenna measuring three feet in diameter and capable of picking up two to six channels. These channels would feature first-run movies, sports and other programs without commercials. A monthly fee of $15 to $20 would be charged, about the same as is charged by most pay-television systems.

Another new mode of television directly involves viewers with what they are watching. Such a system, called Qube, is undergoing market testing in Columbus, Ohio. Qube, a product of Warner Cable Corp., is basically a cable system with an added feature. It is a microprocessor — a small, powerful computer — that permits two-way communication between the viewer and a computer in the Qube offices. Viewers are equipped with a touch pad with five "response buttons," enabling them to respond to questions on the screen about public affairs issues or commercial products or to take part in game shows. Some 30,000 Qube users in Columbus pay a basic charge of $10.95 a month, plus additional fees to watch movies broadcast over the system.

10

Another form of viewer participation is now being tested in Seattle, Wash., where television sets in 200 homes are hooked up to a rating system called VOXBOX. This experimental system is being used by advertisers, including Coca-Cola and United Airlines, to see what volunteer viewers think of their commercial messages. The 562 viewers taking part in the VOXBOX experiment may respond in any one of 12 ways to the commercials. The responses range from "excellent" to "dumb."

Expanding Home Video Market

THE TERM "home video" includes not only the ubiquitous television set, but also video cassette recorders and video disc players — two devices that transmit video programs to a television receiver, giving American consumers the option of watching movies, television or any other video shows whenever they choose. In the case of the video cassette recorders, viewers can also record programs broadcast over the airwaves for later viewing.

The impact of home video on television viewing is being compared to the impact of commercial television broadcasting 35 years ago. More than one million video cassette recorders have been sold in the United States since their commercial introduction in 1976. Next year will mark the widespread introduction of video disc players. This state of affairs "is turning the whole business of television upside down, as advertising wizards, film directors, publishing panjandrums and network chieftains ponder their future in what will be a multibillion-dollar market."[10]

Video tape recorders were first developed in 1956.[11] Twelve years later the Columbia Broadcasting System's Electronic Video Recorder became the first video system to be exhibited and marketed in this country. The CBS video recorders, developed by Peter C. Goldmark, the inventor of the 33-1/3 rpm (revolutions per minute) long-playing record, were sold mainly to industrial and institutional buyers and cost about $800.

Sony Corp., the Japanese firm, introduced the first VCR (video cassette recorder) for home use in this country in 1976. The original Sony Betamax VCR cost $1,300, and had a recording and playing capacity of up to 60 minutes. Sony's initial competition came from another Japanese-based international electronics company, Matsushita Electric Industrial, which released its Video Home Delivery System (VHS) soon after the Sony Betamax was put on the American market. Observers say the

---

[10] Peter J. Schuyten, writing in *The New York Times*, Feb. 17, 1980.
[11] See "Video Revolution," *E.R.R.*, 1971 Vol. I, pp. 227-246.

growth of the video cassette recorder market was hampered by the incompatibility of the two machines — neither could play the other's recordings.

No American electronics company makes its own VCRs; all of those they sell are made by the Japanese. Zenith sells the Sony Beta system; RCA, the other leading American electronics manufacturer, sells the Matsushita VHS type. In all, 19 brand names and 98 models are sold in this country. "You can hardly tell some of them apart," home video expert David Lachenbruch wrote recently, "because all of the models are curently being made by nine Japanese manufacturers: the original Beta-VHS 'big three' — Sony, JVC and Matsushita — joined by Beta followers Sanyo and Toshiba and VHS adherents Akai, Hitachi, Mitsubishi and Sharp."[12]

The video cassette recorder was designed to be used primarily to tape programs for viewing at a later time. Most units come equipped with a remote-control pause button enabling the viewer to edit out commercials. Small electronic timers come installed in all currently available VCRs so that owners may record shows at any time, day or night. Some models can be preset to tape as many as four shows in a seven-day period. Since television signals come to the television receiver through the VCR, the unit can record one program while the viewer is watching another. Newer models have stop-action "freeze" frames, slow motion and visible fast-forward review systems, among other features. Some new models record up to eight hours on one tape. Moreover, color and black-and-white cameras are available for instant-viewing home video recording.

The question of the legality of taping shows off the air has come before the federal courts. Last October, U.S. District Court Judge Warren J. Ferguson in Los Angeles ruled that taping shows on home video (and audio) recorders violates no laws. Ferguson ruled in a case in which Walt Disney Productions and MCA Inc., through its subsidiary Universal Studios, sued Sony Corp. The plaintiffs announced they would appeal the ruling.

Thriving Business in Prerecorded Tapes

While VCRs were originally intended primarily to record home television shows, sales of prerecorded video cassette tapes have become a big business. In the last few years nearly every Hollywood studio has made its films available on video cassettes. *The Video Source Book,* published by the National Video Clearinghouse Inc., lists some 15,000 titles available today. Observers estimate that about one million prerecorded tapes are sold annually in this country.[13]

---

[12] Writing in *Panorama,* February 1980, p. 72.

[13] About six million blank tapes were sold, at an average cost of $20 for a four-hour blank tape.

Best Selling Video Cassettes*

1.	Superman (1978)	$65.00
2.	Grease (1978)	59.95
3.	Blazing Saddles (1974)	55.00
4.	Enter the Dragon (1973)	50.00
5.	The Godfather (1972)	79.95
6.	Saturday Night Fever (1977)	59.95
7.	M*A*S*H (1970)	54.95
8.	The In-Laws (1979)	60.00
9.	Heaven Can Wait (1978)	59.95
10.	Dirty Harry (1971)	55.00
11.	Patton (1970)	74.95
12.	The Exorcist (1973)	60.00
13.	The Godfather, Part II (1974)	79.95
14.	Debbie Does Dallas (1978)	99.50
15.	Deep Throat (1972)	99.50
16.	Butch Cassidy and the Sundance Kid (1969)	54.95
17.	The Wild Bunch (1969)	60.00
18.	Little Girl Blue (1979)	99.50
19.	All the President's Men (1976)	60.00
20.	Halloween (1978)	59.95

* Prerecorded cassettes based on sales figures from a nationwide survey of retail outlets compiled by *Panorama* magazine, May 1980 issue.

The biggest-selling prerecorded items are recently produced motion pictures *(see box, above)*. Feature films sell for $40 to $80. A large share of prerecorded tapes — as many as half, some believe — are X-rated pornographic movies. According to the May issue of *Panorama* magazine,[14] the best-selling prerecorded video cassette was the 1978 movie "Superman," which retails for $65.

Video tape clubs, taking their cue from monthly book clubs, send monthly brochures to members offering selected tapes. VCR owners may also rent tapes for up to $14 per five-day period. Fotomat Corp., the film developing company, now rents video tapes at its 3,700 drive-through outlets. Magazines for VCR owners, including *The Videophile* and *Home Video*, have begun publishing in the last few years. *The Videophile* has a classified advertising section featuring tapes for sale and trade.

One reason for the high price of prerecorded tapes is that each cassette must be recorded individually from a master tape. This is time-consuming and expensive. Industry analysts say that when the technology is developed to make the duplicating process run more efficiently, the retail price will decline. To over-

[14] *Panorama*, a monthly magazine that covers all aspects of television, began publishing in February 1980.

come the cost problem, some VCR owners borrow tapes from public libraries; at least 50 libraries or groups of libraries across the nation now stock prerecorded video cassettes. The libraries in the Chicago system, for example, began lending video cassettes in November 1978 and have made some 20,000 loans since then. The system is receiving about 1,200 requests a month for the 1,000 or so tapes the libraries have in stock.

Coming Introduction of Video Disc Players

The next big development in home video is expected to be the widespread introduction next year of video disc players. After more than a decade of research, home video disc machines went on sale in Europe in 1975. In December 1978, Magnavox started testing the American market by putting them on sale in Atlanta. The Magnavox Magnavision disc player sells for $775, and is available now also in Seattle and Dallas. The Maganavision player is manufactured by the giant Dutch electronics company N. V. Philips in partnership with the American motion picture distributor MCA Inc. RCA, Magnavox's rival in the field, is reported to have spent some $130 million (more than it has spent on any one product, including color television) in developing its own video disc player.

The RCA SelectaVision video disc player is scheduled to be introduced nationally by mid-1981. It will sell for about $500, substantially less than the Maganavox disc player, but will not have such Magnavox features as adaptability for stereo sound, stop action and slow motion. The RCA video disc player, moreover, will be fundamentally different from the Magnavox version. Like the VHS and Beta formats in the video cassette recorder industry, the RCA and Magnavox disc systems are incompatible. The RCA disc player's mechanism is similar to that of a phonograph in that the sound and picture are picked up by a needle which fits into grooves in a disc. The Magnavox system, on the other hand, uses optical laser technology to transmit sound and picture to the television receiver.

Video cassette recorder (front) and disc player

To add to the potential buyer confusion, Japanese manufacturers, including Matsushita[15] and JVC, have been experimenting with a third type of video disc player. Later this year, Sony plans to market a video disc player using the laser projection

---

[15] Matsushita owns the Panasonic and Quasar electronic companies.

system for industrial use, it announced in April. Sony has yet to announce its plans for producing a consumer video disc player.

Since the video disc players do not record, an important factor that will determine the medium's success will be the sale of prerecorded discs. When RCA's video disc players go on sale next year, the company also will have available some 300 programs for sale, half of which will be full-length movies. RCA has contracted with the big motion picture studios, including Paramount, Walt Disney, Twentieth Century-Fox and MGM, for the rights to reproduce recent films on discs. RCA will have available movies like "Annie Hall," as well as old Charlie Chaplin movies, rock concerts, children's shows and sports events. Unlike video cassettes, which can play up to eight hours, RCA discs are limited to only about one hour on each side. But because it is a fairly simple process to stamp out video discs in mass quantities, the price per disc — about $15-20 — will be substantially lower than comparable prerecorded video cassettes.

Magnavox's co-owner, MCA, released an initial disc catalog containing 202 items. Movies such as "American Graffiti" and "Animal House" are available for $24.95 each. Instructional discs sell for as little as $5.95. In the future, first-run movies will be available on both video discs and cassettes. Twentieth Century-Fox announced in March that by 1982 it will release movies on video cassettes and discs to sell to home video viewers at the same time the movies are released to theaters.

Gauging the Marketing Potential for Discs

One way to gauge the future of the video disc business is to look at the number of large corporations that have recently become involved in disc and player production. Zenith Radio Corp., RCA's main rival in the American television and video cassette recorder markets, signed a series of agreements with RCA on March 3 ensuring that both companies' video disc players will be capable of playing the same prerecorded discs. Zenith's disc player is scheduled to go on the market at about the same time as RCA's — sometime in the summer of 1981.

CBS, the nation's leading producer of phonograph records and one of RCA's rivals in network broadcasting, had announced in January that it would produce discs playable only on the RCA format disc machines. Production is due to begin in 1982. IBM last year bought half of MCA's trouble-plagued disc production operation. "IBM efficiency experts and engineers immediately set about improving the operation," David Lachenbruch wrote.[16] In addition, General Motors last year purchased 10,000 custom-made video disc players from Magnavox to use in GM showrooms nationwide. Aside from the $20 million purchase of

---

[16] Writing in *Panorama*, April 1980, p. 59.

the disc players, GM bought 70,000 discs in 1979 and plans to buy 250,000 this year.

Motion pictures make up the bulk of video discs available today. Industry observers say that rock music discs will be big sellers in the future. One reason is that most video disc players have the capability of producing stereo sound and can be hooked easily into home stereo systems. The first full-length rock video disc designed for the commercial market, "Rock Justice," is scheduled to be released this month.[17]

Opinion is divided on whether video discs will achieve great popularity. Richard Sonnenfeldt, an NBC vice president who helped develop RCA's video disc player, has predicted that by 1988 video disc machines will be in 40 percent of the American homes that now have color television.[18] But others say that the incompatibility of the RCA and Magnavox systems will create consumer confusion and severely hamper the industry's growth.

It has been estimated that the manufacturers already have spent more than $1 billion in the development of video disc technology. That large investment should assure that the industry will work diligently to make the discs a success. "By its very nature the video disc must become a mass-market product to exist," David Lachenbruch wrote. "That doesn't mean thousands of players in American homes, but millions — millions per year. In the world of video discs, a small success will be a flop."[19]

Future of Network Television

NEARLY EVERYONE agrees that television will change greatly in the 1980s. But there is no consensus on exactly what impact the changes will have on network broadcasting. ABC, CBS and NBC together earned about $4 billion from advertising revenue in 1979, industry analysts say, and there is concern that more competition will translate into fewer advertising dollars. Some say the increasing popularity of home video and pay-cable may signal the end of network domination of the airwaves. Others contend that the new television modes will boost overall viewing, and bring the networks even more viewers. All agree, as *Business Week* characterized the situation, the networks face "a confusing, misty tomorrow."[20]

---

[17] Written and directed by Bob Heyman and Marty Balin, the former singer with the Jefferson Airplane rock group, the 95-minute rock opera was performed in a San Francisco theater last November. At that time it was videotaped.

[18] See Desmond Smith, "Television Enters the 80's," *The New York Times Magazine*, Aug. 19, 1979.

[19] Writing in *Panorama*, February 1980, p. 118.

[20] "Television's Fragmented Future," *Business Week*, Dec. 17, 1979, p. 60.

Fred Silverman, president and chief execuive officer of NBC, told the California Broadcasters Association last July that by 1988, despite the growth of competing modes, the three networks will keep 90 percent of the audience they now attract. ABC-TV President James E. Duffy told the Executive Club of Chicago on March 21 he was optimistic about network television's future. "Cable TV, home video and the other modes will come primarily as ancillary and add-on services," Duffy said. "I believe the present system will endure and that the 1980s will be its true golden age, with the medium improving steadily in quality and service and doing its best work."[21]

Those thoughts were echoed by Joel Segal, senior vice president of Ted Bates Co., the advertising agency that spends some $260 million a year on television for its clients. He recently told an Association of National Advertisers workshop:[22] "We are confident that ABC, CBS and NBC will be the overwhelmingly dominant video force for years to come," although there will be "small but demographically significant losses by the networks to pay-cable in particular."

Nielsen Survey of Cable Viewing Habits

A.C. Nielsen Co., which measures the size of television audiences, began in February 1979 to study television viewing in homes equipped with pay-cable television. Nielsen has found that some movies and special entertainment shows on pay-cable draw more viewers than some top-rated network shows. "... [W]ithin the households that can receive, say HBO or Show Time, some movies can outdraw the three networks and can do it rather substantially," said Paul Lindstrom, a Nielsen special research marketing coordinator.[23]

"What it basically comes down to is that the people who are watching HBO are people more or less who happen to like television," Lindstrom continued. "It doesn't appear that they are people who are dissatisfied and looking for alternatives. They are the people who . . . are just as likely to flip on the networks as they are HBO or Show Time. . . . It has the effect that within those households instead of having three networks . . . you have four. . . . The good network shows still do well. . . . The low-end network things don't do so well. . . . It just depends on the nature of what's on. If there's a good movie on HBO they'll watch it. If there's a bad one, they won't."

According to Segal of the Ted Bates agency, Nielsen studies have found that those who subscribe to pay-cable are younger and tend to have larger families than those who do not. While

---

[21] Quoted in *Variety*, March 26, 1980.
[22] Held March 26, 1980, at Hilton Head, S.C.
[23] Interview, April 13, 1980.

pay-cable was wired into some 7 percent of the nation's homes in November 1979, 9.4 percent of the persons aged 18-49 subscribed to it. "Furthermore, pay-cable homes view more television not only because there are more viewers in the home but because adults are heavier viewers during prime time and late night when pay is available," Segal said.

Segal added that uncut, adult-rated movies fared very well on cable television. In homes with pay-cable television, according to a sample of prime-time viewing taken last November, the viewers watched network programming 75 percent of the time. Pay-cable viewing was a distant second (12 percent), followed by independent stations (4 percent) and distant independent stations (3 percent). The Public Broadcasting System, superstations and cable-originated programs each accounted for about 1 percent of the viewing time.

Network Investments in New Technology

Some say that the networks will try to meet the new challenges by concentrating on news and sports. "What the networks really can provide now that is not susceptible to [competition from other modes] is a live event — whether it's a live sporting event or whether its a news event," FCC Chairman Ferris told Editorial Research Reports.

All three networks are also working with the new video technologies. ABC and CBS, for example, plan to start new film production departments. "It's obvious that they're thinking about selling those movies some day to pay-cable, cassettes or discs," said Gustave M. Houser, co-chairman, president and chief executive of the combined cable operations of Warner Communicatons and American Express Co. "They see the economics of the business changing. They know that if a subscriber to a cable system likes chess, and the cable operator points a camera at two guys playing a game, the viewer will tune away from a network program and watch it."[24]

RCA, which owns NBC, is heavily involved in the distribution of video cassette recorders and will be among the world's leading manufacturers of video disc players by the end of 1981 *(see p. 339)*. RCA also owns and operates the Satcom I and II satellites that hover 22,300 miles above the equator and beam the fare of the networks' competitors to cable systems throughout the country.[25] Moreover, RCA and NBC are heavily involved in most fields of advanced television technology. "NBC established the first radio networks, NBC was the first television network, NBC

---

[24] Quoted in *Business Week,* Dec. 17, 1979, p. 61.

[25] Each satellite is capable of receiving and sending 24 color TV programs simultaneously. Satcom III, which cost some $77 million, vanished several days after it was launched in December 1979 and has yet to be found.

was the first network to broadcast in color," Fred Silverman said last year, "and I make a pledge: As long as we're here, no matter where the road may be, we'll be the first network to move ahead in the new technology."[26]

CBS, for its part, is working on the development of an information retrieval system called videotext. It would enable people to pay bills, transfer funds from bank accounts, purchase items from catalogs and do a host of other things through electronic manipulations of a home television receiver. Such systems are being developed in European countries, Japan, Hong Kong, Singapore, Australia and Canada. The apparatus is very simple. The viewer uses a hand-held key pad to give instructions to the television receiver. The receiver, in turn, is hooked to a central computer system by a telephone wire or a cable television connection.

The rapid development of alternative broadcasting modes could affect the relationship between the networks and their affiliates. Michael S. Kievman, vice president of broadcast operations for Cox Broadcasting Corp., predicts that in the next decade the networks no longer will pay their affiliates for broadcasting the network programs, as is the case now. Sometime soon, Kievman said, the networks will supply programs to their affiliates only for a fee.

"There won't be any more network exclusivity, but we'll buy services from several networks — just as we do in many of our radio stations, where we carry both Mutual and ABC network programming," Kievman added. "It's going to be a more competitive world but if we're smart enough and pick the right shows, we're going to be highly competitive for a long time to come."[27] According to FCC figures, the networks suffered the net loss of only one affiliate between 1974 and 1978, the last year for which the statistics are complete. As 1979 began, 692 UHF and VHF stations were affiliated with one or another of the networks; 15 other stations were owned and operated directly by ABC, CBS or NBC.

Exactly when a large percentage of Americans will be able to take advantage of the widened television "menu" depends on many factors. If the nation enters a period of severe economic difficulty this year, the capital intensive cable and pay-cable industries might suffer and thus delay the availability of many new television services. Most industry observers agree, though, that massive change in television is inevitable. The main beneficiaries will be the viewers who will be able to enjoy the fruits of television's move from broadcasting to "narrowcasting."

[26] Quoted by Desmond Smith, *op. cit.*, p. 21.
[27] Quoted by Desmond Smith, *op. cit.*, p. 66.

Selected Bibliography

Books

Brown, Les, *Television: The Business Behind the Box,* Harcourt Brace, 1971.
Bower, Robert T., *Television and the Public,* Holt, Rinehart, 1973.
Cunningham, John E., *Cable Television,* Sams, 1976.
MacAvoy, Paul W., ed., *Deregulation of Cable Television,* American Enterprise Institute, 1977.
Phillips, Mary Alice Mayer, *CATV: A History of Community Antenna Television,* Northwestern University Press, 1972.

Articles

Bernstein, Peter W., "Television's Expanding World," *Fortune,* July 2, 1979.
Broadcasting, selected issues.
"Cable TV: The Lure of Diversity," *Time,* May 7, 1979.
Cherry, Susan Spaeth, "Telereference: The New TV Information Systems," *American Libraries,* February 1980.
Clifford, Terry, "Vanity Video," *New York,* Aug. 6, 1979.
Edgerton, Jerry, "Opening Up Your TV," *Money,* December 1979.
Freund, Charles Paul, "Cable TV: The Progress," *Washington Journalism Review,* May 1980.
Matusow, Barbara, "Here Comes Cable TV," *The Washingtonian,* April 1980.
Panorama, selected issues.
Sindermann, Bob Jr., "Cable TV in the Big City: Connections," *The Texas Observer,* Feb. 29, 1980.
Sloan, Allan, "Bring Plenty of Money," *Forbes,* Dec. 10, 1979.
Smith, Desmond, "Mining the Golden Spectrum," *The Nation,* May 26, 1979.
——"Television Enters the 80's," *The New York Times Magazine,* Aug. 19, 1979.
Taylor, Ronald A., "TV Watchers Get an Expanded Menu," *U.S. News & World Report,* April 14, 1980.
"Television's Fragmented Future," *Business Week,* Dec. 17, 1979.

Reports and Studies

Editorial Research Reports: "Broadcasting's Deregulated Future," 1979 Vol. I, p. 165; "Video Revolution: Cassettes and Recorders," 1971 Vol. I, p. 227; "Cable Television: The Coming Medium," 1970 Vol. II, p. 669; "Community Antenna TV," 1964 Vol. II, p. 921.
Tate, Charles, ed., "Cable Television in the Cities," The Urban Institute, 1972.
Zenith Radio Corp., "Annual Report," 1979.

Supreme Court and the Press

by

Elder Witt

**Oct. 26
1 9 7 9**

(**Report update:** The nation's press was breathing somewhat easier at the end of the 1979-1980 Supreme Court term than it had been a year earlier. On the last day of the term, July 2, 1980, exactly a year to the day after its confusing decision in the case of *Gannett v. DePasquale* (p. 25), the court declared that the First Amendment guaranteed press and public a right to attend criminal trials.

This ruling in the case of *Richmond Newspapers v. Virginia* made clear that the Gannett case applied only to the power of a judge in a particular case to close a pretrial hearing. The vote in the Richmond case was 7 to 1. Justice Powell did not participate and Justice Rehnquist dissented.

The major difference between the two cases appeared to be the constitutional basis for the court's reasoning. In *Gannett* the majority had addressed only the question of the Sixth Amendment's guarantee of a public trial, a guarantee they held to apply only to a defendant, not the public or the press. In *Richmond*, the court based its decision on the First Amendment, and there found a constitutional right of citizens and newsmen to obtain information about their government by attending criminal trials.)

SUPREME COURT AND THE PRESS

F ROM the Pentagon Papers to the *Progressive* magazine's atomic secrets case, the 1970s have seen a steady escalation in the tension between the government and the press in the United States. Tension between these two powerful institutions was built into the American system. The press was expected by the Founding Fathers to fill the important function of keeping citizens informed of the workings of the government. But the widespread skepticism and the new activism of journalists during the turbulent years of Vietnam and Watergate spawned an unprecedented number of collisions between the interests of government, the press and society.

A record number of these disputes found their way to the U.S. Supreme Court. From the court, the press in the 1970s has won several notable victories, chief among them the Pentagon Papers case *(see p. 34).* But on balance, the press has lost more cases than it has won. This record has evoked an outpouring of criticism of the court in the press — criticism which Justice William J. Brennan Jr. recently described as containing "a new and disturbing note of acrimony, almost bitterness."[1] For example, the president of the American Newspaper Publishers Association, Allen H. Neuharth, told that organization's convention in April 1979 that the Supreme Court "has battered holes in the First Amendment big enough to drive the whole Constitution through."[2]

Underlying the uneasy relationship between the present court and the press is disagreement over the breadth of the First Amendment's guarantee that "Congress shall make no law . . . abridging the freedom of speech, or of the press. . . ." Does this guarantee set news people apart, granting them special privileges to acquire and publish information? Or does it simply assure every citizen the right to publish or broadcast his views?

Advocates of the first point-of-view, usually members of the institutional media, pointed to an address in 1974 by Justice Potter Stewart, who declared: "[T]he Free Press clause extends protection to an institution. The publishing business is, in short, the only organized private business that is given explicit constitutional protection. . . . The primary purpose of the constitu-

[1] Address at the dedication of the Samuel I. Newhouse Law Center at Rutgers University, Newark, N.J., Oct. 17, 1979.
[2] Address to the 93rd annual convention, American Newspaper Publishers Association, April 23, 1979, in New York.

tional guarantee of a free press was ... to create a fourth institution outside the Government as an additional check on the three official branches."[3]

Among those who espouse the latter view, however, are a majority of Stewart's colleagues on the Supreme Court, including Chief Justice Warren E. Burger. Burger has commented from the bench that he sees "no difference between the right of those who seek to disseminate ideas by way of a newspaper and those who give lectures or speeches and seek to enlarge the audience by publication ... [of their remarks]."[4] Or, as Justice Felix Frankfurter said in an earlier day, "The liberty of the press is no greater and no less than ... the liberty of every citizen of the United States."[5]

Potter Stewart

The current gloomy view among press spokesmen of the contemporary Supreme Court was typified by *Wall Street Journal* reporter Jonathan Kwitny, who wrote last year that "the judiciary ... has for all practical purposes declared war against the press."[6] A few months earlier, the court had held that newspaper offices, including the desks and files of reporters and editors, had no special immunity from police searches. This ruling in the case of *Zurcher v. Stanford Daily* was but a harbinger of things to come.

In November 1978, the justices left standing a contempt citation against *The New York Times* and its reporter M. A. Farber, resulting from their refusal to surrender the notes that Farber had used in writing a series of stories about mysterious deaths among patients in a New Jersey hospital. A doctor was subsequently charged with murder and the defense attorneys sought the notes in preparing their case. Then in another case *(Herbert v. Lando)* the court in April 1979 rejected the argument that the First Amendment protected the "editorial process" — the pre-publication thoughts and conversations of reporter and editor — from inquiry in a libel case *(see p. 26)*.

In June, the court trimmed back the definition of "public figures," those persons who may win damages in a libel suit only if they can prove "actual malice" in the publication. Then, on July 2, the last day of the term, the court upheld, in the case of

---

[3] "Or of the Press," address to the Sesquicentennial Convocation of the Yale Law School, Nov. 2, 1974.

[4] *First National Bank of Boston v. Bellotti,* April 26, 1978, concurring opinion.

[5] *Pennekamp v. Florida,* 328 U.S. 331 (1946).

[6] *The Wall Street Journal,* Aug. 23, 1978, editorial page.

Gannett Co. Inc. v. De Pasquale, a trial judge's decision to keep the press and public out of a pre-trial hearing in a murder case. Afterward, there came this warning from Floyd Abrams, a New York attorney identified with free-press advocacy before the court:

> [I]f some of these trends go ahead . . . we will simply start to lose whole kinds of journalism — it will simply be impossible to report about certain types of things which are terribly important. And that won't mean the end of our freedom, and it won't mean that we are not a free people. . . . But it does mean that we would lose a lot of information which we as citizens . . . have a right to have and ought to have, ought to be able to know about in order to make political rulings of our own. . . .[7]

Fair Trial vs. Free Press in Gannett Ruling

Most controversial of the 1979 rulings was that in the *Gannett* case, upholding the exclusion of press and public from a pre-trial hearing. But that decision drew heavily on the court's earlier rulings emphasizing the responsibility of a trial judge to protect a defendant's right to a fair trial. Justice Stewart, author of the *Gannett* majority opinion, pointed out that the court "has long recognized that adverse publicity can endanger the ability of a defendant to receive a fair trial. . . ." To safeguard the due process rights of the accused, he went on to say:

> [A] trial judge has an affirmative constitutional duty to minimize the effects of prejudicial pre-trial publicity. . . . Closure of pre-trial proceedings is often one of the most effective methods that a trial judge can employ to attempt to insure that the fairness of a trial will not be jeopardized by the dissemination of . . . [inadmissible prejudicial] information throughout the community before the trial itself has even begun.

The Gannett group of newspapers had based its challenge to the closing of the hearing on two constitutional provisions — the Sixth Amendment's guarantee of a public trial and the First Amendment's guarantee of freedom of the press. The First Amendment argument received little attention from the court. The majority — Chief Justice Burger, Justices Stewart, William H. Rehnquist, Lewis F. Powell Jr. and John Paul Stevens — based their decision to uphold the closure order on a literal reading of the Sixth Amendment. It guaranteed only the defendant the right to a public trial, they said; it provided no such guarantee to the press or the public.

Stewart's opinion for the majority seemed to sweep beyond the narrow question of access to a pre-trial hearing to allow judges to close trials as well. But there was disagreement within the majority on that point. Burger added a concurring opinion stating the court had decided only that pre-trial hearings might

---

[7] National Town Meeting, Washington, D.C., Aug. 30, 1979.

be closed. Rehnquist, on the other hand, wrote that a trial judge was now free to close the trial itself, without any explanation, if both the defense and the prosecution agreed that the proceedings should be closed.

In a third concurring opinion, Justice Powell — the only justice to do so — stated that the First Amendment gave newsmen a right to attend pre-trial hearings. In this case, however, Powell said that the judge had fairly weighed that right against the defendant's right and decided to close the hearing.

The dissenters — Justices Brennan, Harry A. Blackmun, Thurgood Marshall and Byron R. White — also based their views on the Sixth, not the First, Amendment. They declared that a pre-trial hearing could properly be closed only in highly unusual circumstances, which were not present in this case. Thus they would overturn the judge's order.

Blackmun wrote for his dissenting colleagues, "The Sixth Amendment, in establishing the public's right of access to a criminal trial and a pre-trial proceeding, also fixes the rights of the press in this regard. Petitioner [Gannett], as a newspaper publisher, enjoys the same right of access to the . . . hearing at issue in this case as does the general public. And what petitioner sees and hears in the courtroom it may, like any other citizen, publish or report consistent with the First Amendment."

Decisions That Widen the Liability for Libel

In 1964, the Supreme Court held for the first time that the First Amendment gave the press some measure of protection against libel suits. The court held, in *The New York Times Co. v. Sullivan,* that when the press is sued for libel as a result of its publication of derogatory information about a public official, the First Amendment requires that the official prove both that the protested report was false and that it was published with "actual malice" — that is, with reckless disregard of its truth or falsity.

Twice in the spring of 1979 the court ruled in cases concerning the use of this standard, and both times against the position taken by the press. In April it ruled on the much-publicized case *(Herbert v. Lando)* involving the Columbia Broadcasting System and Anthony Herbert, a former Army lieutenant colonel. On the CBS "Sixty Minutes" television program, his charges of atrocities in Vietnam were called into question. Herbert sued the network, program producer Barry Lando and reporter Mike Wallace for libel, seeking millions of dollars in damages.

During pre-trial discovery, Lando was questioned extensively by Herbert's attorneys. He answered many of the questions, but refused to respond to those concerning his thoughts and decisions in selecting material to broadcast in the report. He argued that such matters were part of the editorial process, protected from disclosure by the First Amendment.

The Supreme Court disagreed by a vote of 6 to 3. Indeed, wrote Justice White for the majority, such inquiry was mandated by the "actual malice" standard. Writing for himself, Burger, Blackmun, Powell, Rehnquist and Stevens, White explained the *Times* case "made it essential to proving liability that plaintiffs focus on the conduct and state of mind of the defendant. To be liable, the alleged defamer . . . must know or have reason to suspect that his publication is false. . . . Inevitably, unless liability is to be completely foreclosed, the thoughts and editorial processes of the alleged defamer would be open to examination."

". . . A newspaper publisher enjoys the same right of access to the . . . [judicial hearing] as does the general public."

—Justice Blackmun,
dissenting in *Gannett*

Only Stewart of the three dissenters seemed to accept, even in part, the CBS argument that the First Amendment protected the editorial process from such inquiry. Justices Brennan and Marshall would hold that editorial conversations — but not thought processes — enjoyed a limited protection.

In June, two months after the CBS ruling, the court narrowed the category of "public figures" — those persons who must prove "actual malice" in order to recover libel damages. In the case of *Wolston v. Reader's Digest Association Inc.*, the majority held that an individual was not a public figure simply because he was convicted of contempt for failing to appear to testify before a grand jury. Only Brennan dissented.

Justice Rehnquist explained the decision: "A private individual is not automatically transformed into a public figure just by becoming involved in or associated with a matter that attracts public attention. . . . This reasoning leads us to reject the further contention . . . that any person who engages in criminal conduct automatically becomes a public figure for purposes of comment on a limited range of issues relating to his conviction."[8]

The *Wolston* ruling "could be ... quite perilous [for the press]," said magazine writer Nat Hentoff. "If a public figure is only someone who voluntarily thrusts himself into the news, all kinds of non-thrusting newsworthy subjects who feel aggrieved at their treatment by the press will be able to retaliate — if they have deep enough pockets — through libel suits."[9]

Upholding Newsroom Searches; Other Cases

Two decisions in 1978 reaffirmed the court's reluctance to read special privilege into the free press guarantee. In *Zurcher v. Stanford Daily*, the court by a 5-3 vote rejected the argument that the First Amendment obliged police to seek evidence from news organizations through subpoenas. The media argued that a police search such as was conducted at the Stanford University newspaper office — to find evidence identifying participants in a recent demonstration — severely hampered the freedom of the press to gather, analyze and publish information of value to the public.

The court's majority held that freedom of the press was sufficiently protected in such circumstances by the Fourth Amendment's requirement that searches be reasonable and authorized by a specific warrant. The second decision, also from a case *(Houchins v. KQED)* arising in California, rejected a claim that newsmen be granted broader access to prisons and prison inmates than that granted to the public in general. The vote in this case was 4 to 3, with Burger, Stewart, White and Rehnquist forming the majority. Stevens, Brennan and Powell dissented, arguing vigorously that the ruling curtailed a necessary flow of information about the government to the public.

Despite these rulings, the press has had some success in presenting its view to the Supreme Court in recent terms. In 1978, the court held that a state could not constitutionally punish a newspaper for publishing an accurate account of confidential disciplinary proceedings directed at a judge. Although state law mandated the confidentiality of the proceedings, penalizing those who breached it, it could not impose such penalties upon the press.

The court reached this decision by a vote of 7 to 0. Such penalties, Burger wrote in the case of *Landmark Communications v. Virginia,* infringed upon "those interests in public scrutiny and discussion of governmental affairs which the First

---

[8] With similar reasoning, the court held the same day in a companion case *(Hutchinson v. Proxmire)* that a scientist whose federally funded research drew criticism and ridicule as a target of Sen. William Proxmire's "Golden Fleece" award, was not a public figure.

[9] Nat Hentoff, "Libel law: New thorns in the thicket," *Inquiry,* Sept. 10, 1979.

Amendment was adopted to protect." A year later, in June 1979, the court by a vote of 8 to 0 invalidated a West Virginia law which provided for the punishment of a newspaper that published the name of a juvenile charged with a crime. The chief justice also wrote the court's opinion in this case, *Smith v. Daily Mail Publishing Co.*

Free Press and the Constitution

FREEDOM of the press is not simply a privilege granted by idealistic men who drafted the First Amendment. It is an essential factor in the operations of a representative government. Television commentator John Charles Daly has remarked, "Freedom of the press is accepted as the bedrock of a free society on the premise that only an informed public can effectively govern itself."[10]

Thomas Jefferson in 1787 lamented the absence of a free press guarantee in the Constitution drafted that summer in Philadelphia for the new republic. "The people are the only censors of their governors," he wrote, and thus it was necessary that the people be provided "full information of their affairs through the channel of the public papers." In this same letter, he made his famous remark that "were it left to me to decide whether we should have a government without newspapers or newspapers without a government I should not hesitate a moment to prefer the latter."[11] The omission of a free-press guarantee was soon remedied by the addition of a Bill of Rights in 1791.

Almost 200 years later, Justice Lewis F. Powell Jr. reaffirmed Jefferson's view, albeit in a dissenting opinion. "In seeking out the news," he wrote in 1974, "the press therefore acts as an agent of the public at large. It is the means by which the people receive that free flow of information and ideas essential to intelligent self-government. By enabling the public to assert meaningful control over the political process, the press performs a crucial function in effecting the societal purpose of the First Amendment."[12]

Despite the important practical role of a free press in a democratic system, the guarantee of freedom of the press has rarely been viewed as an absolute protection for those who publish information or views distasteful to others.[13] Scholars

---

[10] American Enterprise Institute Forum, "The Press and Public Policy," Jan. 10, 1979, edited transcript, p. 1.

[11] Quoted in Willard Grosvenor Bleyer's *Main Currents in the History of American Journalism* (1927), p. 103.

[12] *Saxbe v. Washington Post*, 417 U.S. 843 (1974).

[13] Two advocates of the absolute view in modern times have been Justices Hugo L. Black (1937-71) and William O. Douglas (1939-75).

generally agree that the men who drafted the First Amendment had in mind Blackstone's definition of freedom of the press, set out some 20 years earlier. He wrote:

> [T]he liberty of the press . . . consists in laying no *previous* restraints upon publications, and not in freedom from censure for criminal matter when published. Every freeman has an undoubted right to lay what sentiments he pleases before the public: to forbid this is to destroy the freedom of the press; but if he publishes what is improper, mischievous, or illegal, he must take the consequences of his own temerity.[14]

Broader View of 1st Amendment Since 1925

The free press guarantee was not interpreted by the Supreme Court until well into this century. There were instances of government restraint upon the press in the 18th and 19th centuries, particularly during wartime, but these restraints were never challenged before the court. Until 1925, the First Amendment was considered to limit only federal — not state — action infringing on freedom of the press. But in that year the court announced in *Gitlow v. New York* that the First Amendment also protected individuals against state action abridging freedom of speech or of the press.

Six years later, in 1931, the court in *Near v. Minnesota* for the first time struck down a state law as abridging freedom of the press. By a vote of 5 to 4 — prophetic of the narrow margins of later press rulings — the court held that Minnesota ran afoul of the First Amendment when it acted to halt publication of a newspaper because it published "scandalous and defamatory matter" about public officials.

Chief Justice Charles Evans Hughes said the state's action was "of the essence of censorship." He continued: "The fact that the liberty of the press may be abused by miscreant purveyors of scandal does not make any the less necessary the immunity of the press from previous restraint in dealing with official misconduct." Subsequent punishment, he added, might be the appropriate remedy for such abuses.

The court in 1936 struck down a Louisiana tax which was intended to apply only to certain large newspapers within the state — newspapers critical of the incumbent governor. Writing for a unanimous court, Justice George Sutherland described the tax as "a deliberate and calculated device . . . to limit the circulation of information to which the public is entitled. . . . A free press stands as one of the great interpreters between the government and the people. To allow it to be fettered is to fetter ourselves."[15]

---

[14] Sir William Blackstone, *Commentaries on the Laws of England,* Vol. 4, pp. 151-153.
[15] *Grosjean v. American Press Co.,* 297 U.S. 233 (1936).

Two years later the court issued the first in a series of rulings protecting the right of individuals to circulate handbills and leaflets. Chief Justice Hughes made clear that the free press guarantee protected more than the institutional press. "The liberty of the press is not confined to newspapers and periodicals. It necessarily embraces pamphlets and leaflets. These indeed have been historic weapons in the defense of liberty.... The press in its historic connotation comprehends every sort of publication which affords a vehicle of information and opinion."[16]

In the seminal opinion in *Near v. Minnesota,* the court emphasized the liability of the press to punishment for publication of defamatory reports, for contempt of court, and for prior restraint in the interest of preserving the national security or the public safety. Since then the court, in every free press case to come before it, has wrestled with the question of whether the circumstances at hand justify punishment of the press — or prior restraint of publication.

Generally, the rulings of the ensuing decades worked to enlarge the freedom enjoyed by the press. By 1968 one scholar would write that "the Supreme Court ... is an assiduous champion of freedom of the press.... It is probably accurate to state that there is greater freedom of the press today than at any time in the history of our republic."[17]

Warren Court Rulings: Times, Sheppard, Hill

During the years (1954-1969) under Chief Justice Earl Warren, the Supreme Court issued several major rulings defining the reach of the First Amendment guarantee of a free press. The first, in 1957, made clear that obscenity still lay outside of that protection.[18] Seven years later, in 1964, the court held that the First Amendment provided the press some protection against libel suits brought by public officials. Writing for the court, Justice William J. Brennan Jr. declared that "[l]ibel can claim no talismanic immunity from constitutional limitations. It must be measured by standards that satisfy the First Amendment."[19]

Until then, the only defense to a charge of libel was proof that the contested statement or report was true. The difficulty and expense of proving truth often operated to prevent the publication of reports likely to provoke retaliatory libel suits. This sort of self-censorship, wrote Brennan, "dampens the vigor and lim-

---

[16] *Lovell v. Griffin,* 303 U.S. 444 (1938).
[17] William A. Hachten, *The Supreme Court On Freedom of the Press: Decisions and Dissents* (1968), pp. 14-15.
[18] *Roth v. United States,* 354 U.S. 476 (1957). For background on obscenity cases, see "Pornography Business Upsurge," *E.R.R.,* 1979 Vol. II, pp. 765-780.
[19] *The New York Times Co. v. Sullivan,* 376 U.S. 254 (1964).

its the variety of public debate" in conflict with the nation's long-held commitment "to the principle that debate on public issues should be uninhibited, robust, and wide-open, and that it may well include vehement, caustic, and sometimes unpleasantly sharp attacks on government and public officials."

The First Amendment, the court declared, required a new standard of proof for libel suits brought by public officials. They could succeed only if the official proved that the defamatory falsehood was made with "actual malice" — that is with the knowledge that it was false or with reckless disregard of its truth or falsity. Because there was no evidence of such "malice" in *The New York Times'* publication of an advertisement describing opposition to the civil rights movement in Montgomery, Ala., the justices unanimously overturned a jury's award of $500,000 in libel damages to that city's police commissioner.

Earl Warren

Later in 1964, the court extended the "actual malice" standard to criminal libel cases in which the state attempted to punish persons or papers that criticized public officials. And in 1967, the court expanded the *Sullivan* ruling to apply it to libel suits brought by public figures as well as by public officials.[20]

In 1967 the Warren Court — over the dissent of the chief justice — applied the *Sullivan* standard to curtail the ability of private individuals to recover damages for invasion of privacy. The court in the case of *Time Inc. v. Hill* overturned a damage award against *Life* magazine as a result of its publishing an article which inaccurately portrayed events occurring during a period in which a family was held hostage by three escaped convicts. The family had sued for invasion of privacy.

But the six-man majority held that the family could recover damages only if they could prove that *Life* published the false portrayal with knowledge of its incorrectness or with reckless disregard of the truth. Writing for the majority, Justice Brennan set out the view that freedom of the press was not restricted to political comment or discussion of public affairs. Individuals who live in a civilized community risk a certain degree of exposure of themselves to others, he wrote; this risk "is an essential incident of life in a society which places a primary value on freedom of speech and of press." To allow publications penalized for innocent or negligent misstatement of facts, such

---

[20] *Garrison v. Louisiana*, 379 U.S. 64 (1964); *Curtis Publishing Co. v. Butts, Associated Press v. Walker*, 388 U.S. 130 (1967).

as those in the article at hand, would discourage the exercise of freedom of the press, he concluded, and so the *Sullivan* standard must apply here.

During the 1960s, it became increasingly apparent that the media, particularly with the growth of television news, posed a serious threat to the right of the individual to a fair trial.[21] The Warren Commission report on events surrounding the assassination of President John Kennedy criticized the actions of newsmen concerning the arrest of Lee Harvey Oswald as characterized by "a regrettable lack of self-discipline." Oswald had effectively been tried and convicted in the press before he, in turn, was killed, the report continued. There are times, the commission wrote, "when the demand for information must be tempered by other fundamental requirements of our society."[22]

In 1961, the court for the first time reversed a state murder conviction because it found that pre-trial publicity had denied the defendant his right to a fair trial.

Warren E. Burger

And in 1965, it reversed the conviction of Texas farmer-financier Billie Sol Estes for swindling, holding that the televising of his trial had denied him his constitutional rights.[23] The following year it ordered the release of Dr. Sam Sheppard, a socially prominent osteopathic surgeon, who was convicted a dozen years earlier of murdering his pregnant wife in their suburban Cleveland home. The "massive, pervasive and prejudicial publicity" surrounding all phases of the Sheppard case had denied him his right to a fair trial. Judges must take "stronger measures," said the court, to ensure that prejudicial publicity did not deny a defendant this right, described in *Estes* as "the most fundamental of all freedoms."[24]

Pentagon Papers; Other Burger Court Cases

Under the leadership of Chief Justice Warren Burger, the Supreme Court has ruled in almost two dozen cases involving freedom of the press. In almost half of those cases, the press has won its argument. The court in the 1970s has steadfastly rejected government efforts to control the content of newspapers or magazines or broadcast reports — through court orders halting publication, "gag" orders or laws requiring newspapers to furnish candidates a "right of reply."

[21] See "Prosecution and the Press," *E.R.R.*, 1967 Vol. II, pp. 481-496.
[22] *Report of the President's Commission on the Assassination of President John F. Kennedy*, pp. 240-242.
[23] *Irvin v. Dowd*, 366 U.S. 717 (1961); *Estes v. Texas*, 381 U.S. 432 (1965).
[24] *Sheppard v. Maxwell*, 384 U.S. 333 (1966).

The present court, however, has been more receptive to arguments of individual privacy and reputation than was the Warren court. It has curtailed the use of the "actual malice" standard in libel cases, most recently in the *Wolston* decision of June 1979. Arguments that the First Amendment gives newsmen special privilege to withhold information — or a special right of access to information — were tried out for the first time on the court of the 1970s,[25] but have met with little success, as the recent rulings in the *Stanford Daily, Herbert* and *Gannett* cases indicate.

The first major press ruling of the Burger era came when the court in June 1971 rebuffed the Nixon administration's effort to halt publication of news stories based on a government history of U.S. involvement in Vietnam, the so-called Pentagon Papers,[26] which was classified "top secret-sensitive." In the case — *New York Times Co. v. United States, United States v. The Washington Post* — the court affirmed that only extraordinary circumstances could justify a prior restraint upon publication of information already in the hands of the newspapers. The court majority found that no such circumstances existed in this case.

A similar case seemed on its way to the court in the current term, arising out of the effort of the government to halt publication by *The Progressive* magazine of an article concerning the making of an H-Bomb. Since the Pentagon Papers decision, two members of that majority (Hugo L. Black and William O. Douglas) and one dissenting justice (John M. Harlan) have left the court and been replaced by other men, sufficient to tip the balance in favor of the government. But the government dropped its case against *The Progressive* after a Wisconsin newspaper, the *Madison Press Connection,* printed information similar to that which the government was trying to keep from disclosure by *The Progressive.*[27]

In 1976, the court for the first time struck down a "gag" order. In this case, *Nebraska Press Association v. Stuart,* it had been issued by a state judge to limit pre-trial reporting of information about a sensational murder in a small town in Nebraska. A unanimous court found such an order too drastic a method of curtailing prejudicial publicity.

In other rulings on government efforts to control the content of

---

[25] See "Newsmen's Rights," *E.R.R.,* 1972 Vol. II, pp. 947-968.

[26] Officially the *History of the United States Decision-Making Process on Vietnam Policy,* a 7,000-page study commissioned by Secretary of Defense Robert S. McNamara. U.S. district courts issued restraining orders preventing stories based on the study from being published by *The New York Times, The Washington Post, The Boston Globe* and the St. Louis *Post-Dispatch.* Only the *Times* and *Post* cases were at issue before the Supreme Court.

[27] For background on the case, see "Atomic Secrecy," *E.R.R.,* 1979 Vol. II, pp. 641-660.

the press the Burger court has upheld a government order
forbidding a newspaper to
publish its help-wanted ads
under sex-related headings,[28]
but it struck down a Florida
law requiring newspapers to
grant political candidates a
right of reply to unfavorable
editorial comment.[29] The
court also has held that a
state may not punish a reporter for broadcasting the
name of a rape victim, once

that name is in public records,[30] but it has allowed a performer
to sue a television station for broadcasting, without his consent,
his entire performance as part of a news show.[31]

Initially, the Burger court seemed comfortable with the Warren court decisions extending the use of the "actual malice"
standard to libel suits brought by private individuals — so long
as those individuals were involved in some matter of public
notice. In 1971, a plurality of the court — including Burger
himself — agreed that this standard should apply to all discussions of public affairs, including those in which defamatory
comments were made about private individuals.[32]

But three years later, with several new members, the court
backtracked and cast Burger into a dissenting role. In the case of
Gertz v. Robert Welch Inc., a 5-4 majority held that a private
citizen could successfully sue for libel without proving actual
malice. In 1976, the court reaffirmed this ruling, stating that an
individual did not become a public figure simply by being
involved in a sensational divorce case.[33] The court's most recent
libel rulings have followed this general trend of narrowing the
category of persons bound to the "actual malice" standard of
proof.

The most publicized and least successful of the free press
cases to come before the Burger court have been those in which
newsmen claim that the First Amendment provides them with
special privileges not enjoyed by the average citizen. The court
has ruled five times against such claims, most recently in the

---

[28] *Pittsburgh Press Co. v. Pittsburgh Commission on Human Relations*, 413 U.S. 376 (1973).
[29] *Miami Herald Publishing Co. v. Tornillo*, 418 U.S. 241 (1974). For background, see "Access to the Media," *E.R.R.*, 1974 Vol. I, pp. 449-470.
[30] *Cox Broadcasting Corp. v. Cohn*, 420 U.S. 469 (1975).
[31] *Zacchini v. Scripps-Howard Broadcasting Co.*, 433 U.S. 563 (1977).
[32] *Rosenbloom v. Metromedia Inc.*, 403 U.S. 29 (1971).
[33] *Time v. Firestone*, 424 U.S. 448 (1976). Mrs. Firestone, who had married into a wealthy and socially prominent family, sued *Time* magazine for incorrectly reporting the grounds upon which the marriage was dissolved.

1978 *Stanford Daily* case and the 1979 *Gannett* case. In each case the outcome was decided by a narrow margin.

In 1972, the court by a 5-4 vote rejected arguments set out in three cases for a First Amendment newsman's privilege, enabling journalists to refuse with impunity to disclose confidential information sought by a grand jury investigating criminal activity. In the cases of *Branzburg v. Hayes, In re Pappas* and *United States v. Caldwell,* reporters argued that their confidential sources would dry up if they were forced to disclose such information to grand juries and prosecutors. Thus, they said, such demands amounted to government infringement upon freedom of the press. The majority, consisting of Burger, White, Blackmun, Powell and Rehnquist, did not agree. They found that the public interest in effective law enforcement outweighed any such burden on freedom of the press.

Two years later, again by 5 to 4 votes, the court upheld state and federal prison rules forbidding newsmen to interview inmates designated by name. "Newsmen have no constitutional right of access to prisons or their inmates beyond that afforded the general public," wrote Justice Stewart for the majority in the cases of *Pell v. Procunier* and *Saxbe v. The Washington Post Co.* Brennan, Marshall, William O. Douglas and Powell dissented.

Chief Justice Burger cited that ruling when the court in 1978 rejected the effort of some California television newsmen to win broader access to a county jail and its inmates than was afforded the general public. The vote in that case, *Houchins v. KQED,* was 4 to 3. Writing for the four-man majority, Burger declared that "[n]either the First Amendment nor Fourteenth Amendment mandates a right of access to government information or sources of information within the government's control." Earlier in the opinion, he said that press representatives, "like all other components of our society . . . are subject to limits."

Balancing of Rights in U.S. Society

THE AMERICAN journalist, *Time* Editor-in-Chief Henry Grunwald wrote last summer, "enjoys unusual latitude and he must, therefore, bear unusual responsibility. He must expect a certain rough-and-tumble in his trade, and not wrap himself in the Constitution at every setback. By no means were all recent court rulings unmitigated disasters. The court in effect allows the press to print anything it can get its hands on."[34]

[34] "Time Essay: The Press, the Courts and the Country," *Time,* July 16, 1979, p. 75.

But it is undeniable that the activities of some newsmen and some news organizations have been made more cautious by the court's rulings. More newsmen have been jailed for contempt, more libel suits will be filed, and more court hearings have been closed than if the court's recent rulings had gone the other way. As of Oct. 15, for example, the Reporters Committee for Freedom of the Press reported that at least 75 requests for closed judicial proceedings had been made since the *Gannett* ruling on July 2, and that 44 had been granted.[35]

The implications of these developments remain unclear. Benjamin C. Bradlee, executive editor of *The Washington Post*, has commented that if the *Stanford Daily* ruling on newsroom searches had been in force during Watergate, "it requires no stretch of the imagination to see police in these [*Washington Post*] offices on a fishing expedition for Messrs. Nixon, Mitchell, Haldeman, Ehrlichman and Company."[36]

"The American journalist . . . must expect a certain rough and tumble in his trade and not wrap himself in the Constitution at every setback."

—Henry Grunwald in *Time*

Jack Landau, director of the Reporters Committee, describes the progression in free press issues during the decade. "You start in 1972 trying to protect a particular source, a specific and narrow matter. And now the court has said that 5,000 documents can be subpoenaed without any showing of necessity, that police can rummage through a whole newsroom, that the government can get reporters' telephone call records for a six-month period,[37] and that editorial thoughts and discussions in a newsroom can be 'seized.' "

Furthermore, he noted, the *Wolston* revision of the definition of a "public figure" called into question the general assumption of most courthouse reporters that anyone involved in a criminal trial was such a figure. And, Landau pointed out, the *Gannett* ruling allows the press to be shut out of pre-trial hearings — where 89 percent of all indictments are disposed of in such hearings.[38]

---

[35] "Court Watch Study," compiled by The Reporters Committee for Freedom of the Press, updated as of Oct. 15, 1979.

[36] Quoted in *U.S. News & World Report*, June 12, 1978, p. 40.

[37] *Reporters Committee for Freedom of the Press v. American Telephone & Telegraph Co.*, review denied, March 5, 1979.

[38] Figure cited in *amicus curiae* (friend of the court) brief (p. 19) filed in the *Richmond Newspapers v. Virginia* case by the Reporters Committee and seven other journalistic organizations.

After the Supreme Court refused in 1972 to read a "newsman's privilege" into the First Amendment, Congress considered enacting legislation specifically granting journalists such a right. Hearings, however, revealed considerable disagreement over the scope of such a legislative privilege, even within the ranks of working journalists. As Grunwald recently remarked, "spelling out rights that were assumed to exist under the general protection of the First Amendment may very well result in limiting those rights." A number of states did enact such legislation, with varying results. A newsman's privilege law enacted by New Jersey did not keep M. A. Farber out of jail, for example.

After the *Stanford Daily* decision in 1978, the Carter administration proposed legislation forbidding police to use search warrants to obtain reporter's notes, photographs, tapes or other "work products." As of October 1979, such legislation was still in committee — along with a broader bill introduced in mid-September by Sen. Birch Bayh, D-Ind., chairman of the Senate Judiciary Subcommittee on the Constitution. At the American Bar Association's 1979 convention, however, the ABA board of governors rejected a motion to endorse the Carter administration's bill. One practical aid to newspapers faced with an increasing number of First Amendment problems has been developed with the encouragement of the American Newspaper Publishers Association. The Mutual Insurance Co. of Bermuda, a company that insures papers against libel losses, has announced that it will also offer up to $1 million in insurance for legal fees that might be incurred in First Amendment cases.

Prospect of New Justices and Interpretations

The finality of some of the Supreme Court's press rulings is called into question by the narrow margins by which they have been obtained. The switch of one vote often would have rendered an entirely different decision. Since five of the nine justices are 70 or older, and some have encountered health problems in recent years, there is a clear possibility of new faces on the court after this term. Of the five, Brennan and Marshall have been the court's only two consistent liberals. The other three (Burger, Blackmun and Powell) are all appointees of President Nixon. The last justice to be named to the court was John Paul Stevens, in 1975; not since the 1930s has the court gone so long without a change in its membership.

And sitting justices can change their minds. Stewart was considered one of the justices more kindly disposed toward the press, after his 1974 speech advocating an institutional privilege under the First Amendment. Yet in 1979, Stewart was the author of the controversial and confusing *Gannett* decision.

In a highly unusual public display of internal disagreement, four of the justices (Burger, Stevens, Blackmun and Powell) spoke out last summer to give their views on the interpretation of that ruling. The court may clarify the issue further in a case to be argued in the current term, which began Oct. 1. In the case of *Richmond Newspapers v. Virginia,* the press challenges the decision of a trial judge to exercise his power under state law to exclude press and public from a murder trial. The newspapers argue that the judge did not sufficiently weigh the First and Sixth Amendment interests in a free press and a public trial. In a friend-of-the-court brief filed in that case, the Reporters Committee, backed by a number of other press organizations, urged the court to overturn *Gannett.*

Warnings That the Press Has Overreacted

Robert M. Kaus, writing in *The Washington Monthly,* sees as the unifying element in the recent court rulings an attack "on the idea that the press, and the people who work in the press, enjoy constitutional protection unavailable to ordinary citizens." Kaus adds that "as an ordinary citizen, I appreciated that sentiment, and it seemed to me that much of the outcry was only journalists' anger at being stripped of their pretensions to special treatment."[39]

Vermont Royster, former editor of *The Wall Street Journal,* has sounded a similar note, writing that the press "should be wary of giving an impression that we and our government are adversaries because it is upon press and government together that all our liberties depend. We should be especially wary of claiming for ourselves alone exemptions from the obligations of all citizens, including the obligation to bear witness once due process has been observed. There is nothing in the Bill of Rights, including the First Amendment, that makes the press a privileged class apart."[40]

Justice Brennan, in a recent speech, warned the press to lower its voice. He urged the press to "tailor its arguments and its rhetoric" more carefully to the precise situation at hand. "This may involve a certain loss of innocence, as certain recognition that the press, like other institutions, must accommodate a variety of important social interests. But the sad complexity of our society makes this inevitable, and there is no alternative but a shrill and impotent isolation. These are hard words, but there is much at stake, not the least of which is the ability of the press to resume its sure voice as a reliable conscience of this nation."

---

[39] "The Constitution, the Press, and the Rest of Us," *The Washington Monthly,* November 1978, p. 51.

[40] "Reflections on the Fourth Estate," *The Wall Street Journal,* Dec. 13, 1978, editorial page.

Selected Bibliography

Books

Brant, Irving. *The Bill of Rights: Its Origin and Meaning,* Bobbs-Merrill, 1965.

Cater, Douglass. *The Fourth Branch of Government,* Houghton Mifflin Co., 1959.

Emerson, Thomas I., *The System of Freedom of Expression,* Random House, Vintage Books, 1970.

——*Toward A General Theory of the First Amendment,* Random House, 1963, 1966.

Hachten, William A., *The Supreme Court on Freedom of the Press: Decisions and Dissents,* Iowa State University Press, 1968.

Hiebert, Ray Eldon (ed.), *The Press in Washington,* Dodd, Mead & Co., 1966.

Wicker, Tom, *On Press,* Viking Press, 1978.

Witt, Elder (ed.), *Guide to the U.S. Supreme Court,* Congressional Quarterly Inc., 1979.

Articles

American Enterprise Institute Forum, "The Press and Public Policy," Jan. 10, 1979.

——"The Press and the Courts: Competing Principles," Oct. 3, 1978.

Anderson, David A., "Libel Law Today," *Trial,* May 1978.

Grunwald, Henry, "The Press, The Courts and the Country," *Time,* July 16, 1979.

Hentoff, Nat, "Libel Law: New Thorns in The Thicket," *Inquiry,* September 1979.

Kaus, Robert M. "The Constitution, the Press, and the Rest of Us," *The Washington Monthly,* November 1978.

Kinsley, Michael, "Journalists' Privilege," *The New Republic,* May 12, 1979.

Rubin, David M., "Reporters, Keep Out!" *Columbia Journalism Review,* March-April 1979.

Sanford, Bruce W., "No Quarter From This Court," *Columbia Journalism Review,* September-October 1979.

Tavoulareas, William P., "Freedom of the Press — License to Hurt?" *Saturday Review,* April 28, 1979.

"An Anti-Press Backlash in Courts?" *U.S. News & World Report,* June 12, 1978.

Reports and Studies

Editorial Research Reports: "First Amendment and Mass Media," 1970 Vol. I, p. 43; "Prosecution and the Press," 1967 Vol. II, p. 481; "Access to the Media," 1974 Vol. I, p. 449; "News Media Ownership," 1977 Vol. I, p. 185; "Media Reformers," 1977 Vol. II, p. 975.

Atomic Secrecy

by

William Sweet

Sept. 7
1 9 7 9

(**Report update:** On Sept. 17, 1979, following publication of an article on H-bomb design in the *Madison Press Connection,* the Justice Department announced it was dropping its effort to bar publication of Howard Morland's article in *The Progressive* magazine. The Justice Department left open the possibility, however, that it might file criminal charges against those who had exposed information about hydrogen bombs.

In the intervening months, lawyers for *The Progressive* have conducted negotiations with the Justice Department concerning what materials connected with the magazine's defense are to remain under lock and key. It had been expected that a formal agreement would be reached in a court hearing on July 16, 1980, in Milwaukee, Wis. But *The Progressive* refused at that hearing to sign a stipulation until the government specifies whether it still plans to file criminal charges, and a new hearing is scheduled for Sept. 4.

The magazine fears that some of the scientists who assisted in its defense may be prosecuted, and it is unwilling to sign away documents that might be needed in their defense. Meanwhile in Congress, the House Subcommittee on Government Information and Individual Rights has been holding hearings on atomic secrecy. It is considered likely that the subcommittee will recommend at the end of the summer a change in the law which declares all atomic information secret unless or until the government says otherwise.)

ATOMIC SECRECY

O N SEPT. 13 the U.S. Court of Appeals in Chicago is scheduled to hear what already is being spoken of as an "historic" and "landmark" case, placing First Amendment rights onto a collision course with federal atomic secrecy law. The case pits the U.S. government against *The Progressive* magazine, its editors, Erwin Knoll and Samuel Day Jr., and Howard Morland. Morland is the author of an article which Knoll and Day had planned to publish earlier in the year under the title "The H-Bomb Secret: How We Got It, Why We're Telling It." The government learned of their intention to print the article in late February, and after failing to persuade them to voluntarily delete roughly 20 percent of the text and all of the diagrams showing how an H-bomb works, requested a court injunction against publication. Acting under the Atomic Energy Act of 1954, U.S. District Court Judge Robert W. Warren granted the government's request on March 26.

Warren said he agonized over the decision, which he characterized as "the first instance of prior restraint against a publication in this fashion in the history of this country." But Warren said he had no choice but to decide in favor of the government because to rule otherwise "could pave the way for nuclear annihilation for us all." Lawyers for *The Progressive* promptly appealed the decision, arguing that the sweeping secrecy provisions of the Atomic Energy Act are in violation of the First Amendment, which permits no law abridging freedom of the press.

The reactions of the press to *The Progressive* case have been highly ambivalent. Many newspapers editorialized in favor of the government, especially during the weeks immediately after the court injunction was imposed. *The Washington Post,* for example, called it "John Mitchell's dream case," arguing that the Nixon administration would have liked to have gotten a case so likely to result in curtailed freedom of the press.[1] In recent months, however, many publications have come around to support *The Progressive.* The board of the American Society of Newspaper Editors reluctantly voted 16-0 in early May to file a friend-of-the-court brief on behalf of the magazine. Friend-of-the-court briefs on behalf of *The Progressive* also have been filed

---

[1] *The Washington Post,* March 11, 1979.

by other publications and organizations, including *The New York Times,* the *Chicago Tribune, Scientific American,* the Association of American Publishers, the National Association of Broadcasters, *Playboy,* and *The New Republic.*

Whatever the Court of Appeals ultimately decides, the loser — whether it is the government or the magazine — will almost surely appeal the ruling to the U.S. Supreme Court. While the Supreme Court could conceivably decline to hear the case, it is unlikely to do so in a case involving two issues as important as atomic secrecy and prior censorship. Chief Justice Warren E. Burger stressed in his dissenting opinion in the 1971 Pentagon Papers case, which frequently is compared with *The Progressive* case, that there is a strong presumption against the validity of prior restraints on publication.

"So clear are the constitutional limitations on prior restraints against expression," Burger said, "that ... we have had little occasion to be concerned with cases involving prior restraints against news reporting on matters of public interest. There is, therefore, little variation among the members of the court in terms of resistance to prior restraints against publication." Burger went on to state, however, that prior restraints may be necessary in some instances. When "the imperative of a free and unfettered press comes into collision with another imperative," he said, the case is "simple or easy" only for "those who view the First Amendment as an absolute in all circumstances." "First Amendment absolutism," Justice Harry A. Blackmun pointed out in the same decision, "has never commanded a majority of this court."[2]

Many people believe instinctively that if any imperative warrants abridgment of First Amendment rights, it is that of preventing nuclear war. But the editors of *The Progressive* argue that the H-bomb article reveals no secrets which could add to the risk of nuclear war. In fact, they claim that publication of the article would enhance prospects for world peace.

Origins of the Howard Morland Article

The Progressive, a magazine with a long tradition of political muckraking, was founded in 1909 as *La Follette's Weekly Magazine* by Sen. Robert M. La Follette of Wisconsin. La Follette, the Progressive Party's candidate for president in 1924, was the leading opponent of U.S. participation in World War I. Erwin

[2] *New York Times Company v. United States,* 403 US 713 (1971). At issue was the publication, first by *The New York Times* and later by several other newspapers, of excerpts from a Department of Defense classified study entitled "History of U.S. Decision-Making Process on Viet Nam Policy." The court decided in favor of the paper, holding that the government had not shown justification for enforcement of a restraint. For background on the case and First Amendment law, see "Secrecy in Government," *E.R.R.,* 1971 Vol. II, pp. 627-650, and "First Amendment and Mass Media," *E.R.R.,* 1970 Vol. I, pp. 41-60.

H-Bomb Article Chronology

Mid-1978. Samuel H. Day Jr., the managing editor of *The Progressive,* tours nuclear weapons production facilities for an article.

June 1978. Day meets Howard Morland at an anti-nuclear demonstration, encourages him to do series of articles on secrecy in nuclear weapons production.

July 28, 1978. Morland informs Department of Energy (DOE) of intention to do series.

Feb. 15, 1979. George W. Rathjens, a professor at the Massachusetts Institute of Technology, informs Day that Morland's article contains secret material.

Feb. 16. *Progressive* learns Rathjens has sent article to DOE classification officer.

Feb. 21. Day sends sketches and captions from Morland manuscript to DOE public affairs officer James S. Cannon with request that he comment on their accuracy.

Feb. 26. Day calls Cannon and learns that sketches have not been received; sends entire manuscript to Cannon that day by express mail.

Feb. 28. DOE lawyers inform Justice Department that manuscript contains secret data.

March 2. *Progressive* editors meet with DOE and Justice officials, who request voluntary deletion of about 20 percent of article's text and diagrams.

March 6. Editors send to press April issue of *Progressive,* without H-bomb article and including instead an alternative article and cover.

March 7. *Progressive* lawyers inform DOE counsel that unless the United States promptly obtains a temporary restraining order, the magazine will proceed with publication of the article.

March 8. Government lawyers file for court injunction.

March 9. U.S. District Court Judge Robert W. Warren issues 10-day restraining order.

March 26. Judge Warren issues preliminary injunction barring *Progressive* from printing and distributing H-bomb article.

May 7. Dimitri A. Rotow, a volunteer researcher for the American Civil Liberties Union (ACLU) finds a document — UCRL 4725 — containing H-bomb secrets on open shelves at Los Alamos Scientific Library.

May 11. Los Alamos Scientific Library closed to the public.

May 23. Sen. John Glenn, D-Ohio, discloses a second declassified document — UCRL 5280 — revealing supposedly secret material on H-bomb.

June 8. Justice Department files stipulation with Judge Warren that a competent scientist who had read UCRL 5280 would get "no significant additional information or benefit" from Morland article.

July 2. Supreme Court declines to order expedited appeal hearing for *Progressive.*

Knoll, who became editor of *The Progressive* in 1973, previously had been White House correspondent for the Newhouse Newspapers and Washington editor of the Los Angeles Times-Washington Post News Service. Samuel Day joined the magazine as managing editor in 1978 after leaving *The Bulletin of the Atomic Scientists,* where he developed an interest in the nuclear weapons production industry.[3]

In the summer of 1978 Day met free-lance writer Morland, who also was interested in nuclear weapons production. Day encouraged him to do a series for *The Progressive.* Morland agreed and, in a letter to the magazine dated July 7, 1978, he stated his understanding that the series should "raise the visibility of the nuclear warhead assembly line, which stretches in a great arc across America," and further, that the H-bomb — the most potent weapon in the U.S. arsenal — should be described in enough detail "to allow readers to see nuclear warheads as pieces of hardware rather than as score-points in a contest."[4]

Upon conveying his intentions to the Department of Energy (DOE), which is responsible for nuclear weapons research, development, testing and production, Morland obtained the agency's permission to visit production facilities. In February 1979, Morland published the first article of his series in *The Progressive.*[5] Around the same time the magazine prepared to go into print with his article on the H-bomb. The article showed, according to Day, how knowledge of each major aspect of design is essential to assessing various policy issues, such as the pros and cons of a comprehensive test ban treaty.[6]

According to sworn affidavits Morland has submitted in court, he developed his article exclusively on the basis of publicly available literature and interviews with people who knew of his intentions. Judging from the affidavits, what he came up with was much less detailed than a "blueprint" for a bomb but much more detailed than just "the general idea" of a bomb.[7] Large portions of the affidavits have been censored, however, along with background materials he used for the article, includ-

---

[3] Interview, Aug. 22, 1979. *The Bulletin* is published by The Educational Foundation for Nuclear Science, Inc., in Chicago, Ill.

[4] Erwin Knoll, "Born Secret," *The Progressive,* May 1979, p. 12.

[5] Howard Morland, "Tritium: The New Genie," *The Progressive,* February 1979, pp. 20-24. The article discusses U.S. production of tritium, a rare form of hydrogen which is an important ingredient in H-bombs *(see box, p. 53).*

[6] Interview, Aug. 22, 1979.

[7] See especially Affidavit I of Howard Morland in Opposition to Motion for Preliminary Injunction, U.S. District Court for the Western District of Wisconsin, Civil Action No 79-C-98.

ing his underlined passages in the 1977 *Encyclopedia Americana* article on the hydrogen bomb written by Dr. Edward Teller, the physicist who is thought of as the father of the H-bomb.

On Feb. 16 *The Progressive* learned that a professor at the Massachusetts Institute of Technology had forwarded the Morland manuscript to DOE. There followed the chain of events, summarized on p. 45, which led to imposition of a court injunction and to a flurry of controversy over what prompted the magazine to publish an article on H-bomb design.

Author's Motives, Defense of Publication

Morland, a former Air Force pilot, has been concerned in recent years about nuclear arms. He believes many members of the anti-nuclear power movement really are more concerned about weapons than about reactors, but they seem to think you "can't fight the Pentagon" and that it is "easier to fight a local utility."[8] The reason people feel helpless in the face of the Pentagon, Morland argues, is that they are "afraid to acquire knowledge." Morland thinks the fear is carefully nourished by members of the nuclear weapons establishment who cultivate "the secret" in order to maintain their monopoly on power.

To those who say they do not need to know how a bomb works to make judgments about defense policy, Morland suggests they try to imagine that the workings of the internal combustion engine were a state secret. "Imagine what a chilling effect that would have on public debate on the contribution of the internal combustion engine to air pollution, to the fuel crisis, to whether we have mass transit or build more highways," he argued.[9]

Others contend that no policy issue warrants release of information about hydrogen bomb design to the general public. Jeremy J. Stone, director of the Federation of American Scientists (FAS), said that there is "no plausible reason why supporters of the test ban are hampered by not knowing technical details of how the bomb is built."[10] But *The Progressive* claims that atomic secrecy has impeded public discussion in many cases. In Hawaii, for example, citizens' groups recently discovered that the U.S. Navy was planning to store nuclear

---

[8] Interview, Aug. 3, 1979.

[9] Debate with Reid Irvine, Chairman of Accuracy in Media (AIM), June 14, 1979, available from Committee to Defend the First Amendment, Washington, D.C., p. 37. Accuracy in Media is an organization that monitors press and television news reporting. While it calls itself a watchdog group devoted to promoting "fairness in reporting on critical issues," others have accused it of allowing a politically conservative bias to color its judgments. See "Media Reformers," *E.R.R.*, 1977 Vol. II, pp. 81-100.

[10] *F.A.S. Public Interest Report*, May 1979, p. 2.

weapons one mile north of the main runway at Honolulu International Airport. When they went to court to demand an environmental impact statement for the plan, a DOE classification officer testified that the Navy could not submit a statement because this would violate data restrictions of the Atomic Energy Act of 1954. The judge ruled that the government did not have to submit the environmental impact statement.[11]

Government Arguments Against Disclosure

The Atomic Energy Act of 1954 makes it illegal to communicate, transmit, or disclose restricted data to any individual or person, with intent to injure the United States or "with reason to believe such data will be utilized to injure the United States or to secure an advantage to any foreign nation." The term "restricted data" covers all information concerning: (1) design, manufacture, or utilization of atomic weapons; (2) the production of special nuclear material (mainly plutonium and enriched uranium); or (3) the use of special nuclear material in the production of energy, but does not include data declassified or removed from the restricted data category.[12] Any information pertaining to the design, manufacture, or use of atomic weapons or to the production of atomic energy is automatically classified unless the government says otherwise. Restricted data, including original ideas about atomic energy, are "classified at birth."

The government asserts that some information contained in Morland's article is restricted irrespective of whether he obtained it from open sources or not, and communication of that information would make it easier for other countries or organizations to build H-bombs. According to a sworn affidavit submitted by Secretary of Defense Harold Brown, "A country or a subnational element [a terrorist or criminal group] within a country that had the technical capability to develop and produce an unsophisticated fission-type nuclear explosive [an A-bomb] would gain technical assistance in determining the appropriate direction to pursue in developing high yield thermonuclear explosives [H-bombs]."[13] The government has not revealed, for obvious reasons, what information in Morland's article would help speed up a country's hydrogen bomb development. But it is generally assumed that the information has something to do with the Teller-Ulam design ideas which cleared the way for production of the first U.S. hydrogen bomb (see p. 54).

---

[11] See *The New York Times*, June 3, 1979.
[12] Atomic Energy Act of 1954, *U.S. Code: Congressional and Administrative News*, 83d Congress, Second Session, 1954, p. 1124 and p. 1082.
[13] Reprinted in *The Progressive*, May 1979, p. 36.

Civil libertarians argue that the sweeping language of the Atomic Energy Act, and the manner in which the government is trying to apply it, would mean that anybody wishing to publish lawfully acquired knowledge about nuclear weapons or atomic energy first must obtain permission from the government. "Advance licensing of publications is the essence of censorship," Nathan Lewin wrote in *The New Republic,* and "it is clear that the founding fathers intended to prohibit this censorship with the adoption of the First Amendment."[14] Civil libertarians warn that terrible consequences would follow from a ruling upholding the government's position. Suppose, they say, the government put U.S. nuclear forces on alert, as President Nixon did during the 1973 Middle East war, at a time when Watergate was the national preoccupation. On the government's interpretation of the Atomic Energy Act, in a situation of this kind it could classify all information about the alert, refuse to explain the reasons for it, and seek court injunctions against any newspaper or network communicating information about the alert.

However dangerous consequences of this kind may be, defenders of the government argue that the courts can be and must be trusted to apply the Atomic Energy Act with discrimination and to protect legitimate political speech. The injunction against *The Progressive,* they point out, is the only instance in which censorship has been imposed under the act. And distribution of Morland's H-bomb diagrams, far from representing legitimate political speech, is more properly seen — according to this line of reasoning — as comparable to the act of a pornographer who circulates dirty pictures to promote free love.

Access to Atomic Data Since 1939

G ERMAN scientists working in Berlin discovered nuclear fission — the splitting of an atomic nucleus which results in the release of large amounts of energy — in late 1938. News spread rapidly around the world and the possibility of creating a new kind of weapon of unprecedented explosive force was widely recognized. A debate ensued among scientists as to whether they should continue to publish atomic research results, but initially there was strong resistance to the idea of secrecy among people whose work had depended for decades on the free exchange of information. With the outbreak of World War II, however, fears grew that Germany might be the first country to

---

[14] Nathan Lewin, "How a Legal Bomb Works," *The New Republic,* March 24, 1979, p. 12.

build an atomic bomb. In April 1940 U.S. scientists agreed among themselves not to publish papers which might be of help to Germany, and with the establishment of the Manhattan Project in August 1942, a tight system of government security was imposed on atomic weapons research.

The more free-wheeling scientists on the Manhattan Project felt classification procedures were a considerable annoyance. J. Robert Oppenheimer, the head of the Los Alamos laboratory where the bomb itself was being designed, squabbled repeatedly about security measures and his past associations with communists with Maj. Gen. Leslie R. Groves, the military manager of the project. But the basic rationale for secrecy was generally accepted.

Nonetheless, the early results of atomic secrecy appear to have been ambiguous. The American public was kept in the dark about the Manhattan Project, and in 1945 the atomic bomb was used against Japan without public debate or consent. Russia, on the other hand, got wind of the project early on. The discovery by Russian scientists that their American counterparts had stopped publishing led them to assume that a secret A-bomb project had been started *(see p. 51)*. At least one spy, Klaus Fuchs, a scientist who had joined hte project as part of the British team, provided the Soviet Union with information on what the Manhattan scientists were up to.

Manhattan Project secrecy may have been more effective in retarding German progress in atomic development. The Germans apparently were working along unpromising lines, and while they claimed after the war that they had misdirected their research in order to avoid giving Hitler the bomb, that notion now is said to be "discredited."[15] Undoubtedly the main reason why the United States beat both Germany and Russia to the bomb, however, was that it alone could afford under wartime conditions to finance a massive industrial and scientific effort which might well produce no usable results before the war ended.

1946 Atomic Energy Act and Its Effects

Soon after World War II ended, a controversy erupted over how the use of atomic energy should be controlled. A bill introduced in Congress in October 1945, the May-Johnson bill, would have left considerable control over nuclear power with the military.[16] Scientists associated with the Manhattan Project

---

[15] David Holloway, "Entering the Nuclear Arms Race: The Soviet Decision to Build the Atomic Bomb, 1939-45," International Security Studies Program, The Wilson Center, Working Paper No. 9, 1979, p. 50.

[16] The bill was introduced by Sen. Edwin C. Johnson, D-Colo., and Rep. Andrew J. May, D-Ky.

Influence of U.S. Secrecy on Soviet A-Bomb Program

End 1938. Discovery of nuclear fission by Otto Hahn and Fritz Strassmann in Berlin

Jan. 1939. Niels Bohr informs scientists at Princeton, N.J., of the discovery of fission

Feb. 1939. Soviet scientists learn of the discovery of fission from foreign science journals

Aug. 1939. Albert Einstein writes to FDR warning of A-bomb possibility

Late 1940 (or early 1941). Russian scientist N. N. Semenev writes to Soviet government warning of A-bomb possibility

April 1940. U.S. scientists agree not to publish papers that might help Germany develop A-bomb

June 1940. FDR organizes National Defense Research Committee, headed by Vannevar Bush, and gives it jurisdiction over uranium research

June 1941. Germany invades Soviet Union; Russian uranium research suspended

1942. Soviet State Defense Committee names S. V. Kaftanov "plenipotentiary" for science and sets up Scientific-Technical Council to assist him

Dec. 1941. Vannevar Bush recommends, the day before Pearl Harbor, launching a crash program to build the bomb

Fall 1942. Scientist G. N. Flyorov writes to Stalin that lack of publications from top U.S. scientists indicates secret A-bomb project; Kaftanov recommends resumption of uranium research

Aug. 1942. U.S. A-bomb project, the "Manhattan Project," is established; Maj. Gen. Leslie R. Groves made head in Sept.

Oct. 1942. Soviet A-bomb project established, and Igor Vasil'evich Kurchatov — a top nuclear physicist — agrees to head it up

Source: David Holloway, "Entering the Nuclear Arms Race: The Soviet Decision to Build the Atomic Bomb, 1939-45," Working Paper No. 9, International Security Studies Program, The Woodrow Wilson Center, Washington, D.C., 1979.

lobbied hard for an alternative bill introduced by Sen. Brien McMahon, D-Conn., and Rep. Helen Gahagan Douglas, D-Calif., and they won. The Atomic Energy Act of 1946 put control of atomic energy in the hands of a civilian Atomic Energy Commission (AEC) and gave oversight authority to a Joint Committee on Atomic Energy.

The Atomic Energy Act imposed rigid restrictions on transferring atomic information to other countries and, in effect, cut off wartime allies who had contributed to the Manhattan Project from what they saw as the fruits of their efforts. These restrictions may have retarded Britain and France's efforts to build atomic weapons of their own. On the other hand, some believe the British and French leaders perceived the restrictions as a violation of wartime agreements and thus became all the more determined to have nuclear programs of their own.

At the root of the restrictions was the hope that secrecy would prevent Russia, which was emerging as America's Cold War adversary, from developing atomic weapons for many years. Some scientists sought to convince the public that Russia would need no more than a few years to design a bomb. But many people were predisposed to regard the bomb as a uniquely American achievement, and they were inclined to believe experts like Maj. Gen. Groves, who testified that the Soviet Union might need as much as 20 years to build a bomb.

Soviet A-Bomb and the U.S. H-Bomb

News that the Soviet Union had tested an atomic bomb, which President Truman announced Sept. 23, 1949, came as a tremendous shock. Truman himself refused to announce the test until his science advisers had signed sworn statements saying they really believed the Russians had done it.[17] The Soviet Union had taken just four years to build the bomb from the time it launched an all-out effort, only five months more than it had taken the United States.

Truman's decision to proceed with development of a hydrogen bomb, which he announced Jan. 31, 1950, is perhaps best understood in terms of public anxiety over Soviet power. It had been recognized before 1945 that it might be possible to build a bomb in which a fission explosive (an A-bomb) could be used to create the heat and pressure necessary to start a fusion reaction, the type of reaction which takes place in the sun *(see p. 53)*. A fusion bomb — or hydrogen bomb, as it came to be known — would be much more powerful than an A-bomb, and in fact there would be no upper limit on how powerful a bomb could be built. But while it had been relatively easy to demonstrate the feasibility of building an A-bomb, the feasibility of an H-bomb was much harder to prove, and from 1946 to 1950 much of the work at Los Alamos was focused on just this problem.[18] The work involved enormously complicated calculations, and progress went hand in hand with development of the electronic computer.

---

[17] Herbert F. York, *The Advisors: Oppenheimer, Teller, and the Superbomb* (1976), p. 34.

[18] J. Carson Mark, "A Short Account of Los Alamos Theoretical Work on Thermonuclear Weapons, 1946-1950," U.S. Atomic Energy Commission, July 1974, p. 10.

Exploding a Hydrogen Bomb

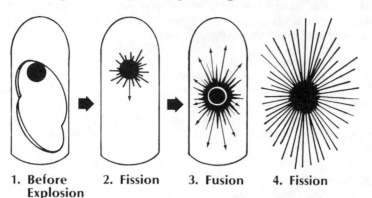

1. **Before Explosion**   2. **Fission**   3. **Fusion**   4. **Fission**

1. A fission bomb (A-Bomb) containing TNT and Uranium-235 (a highly fissionable isotope of uranium) is used to trigger a thermonuclear or fusion explosion (H-Bomb). Fission is the splitting apart of the nucleus of a heavy atom, such as uranium — a process that releases energy. In a fusion explosion, energy is released when two atoms of a lighter element, such as hydrogen, are joined together to form one heavier atom, such as helium.
2. Detonation of the TNT compresses the U-235 and causes it to undergo fission; neutrons are released and the temperature rises to millions of degrees Celsius.
3. The fission bomb trigger is surrounded by a compound of lithium, a very light metal, and deuterium, a form of hydrogen that has extra neutrons. Neutrons from the fission explosion hit the lithium nuclei, transforming them into helium and tritium, another form of hydrogen that contains extra neutrons. Tritium fuses with the deuterium to form more helium. This releases the extra neutrons contained in the two forms of hydrogen.
4. Some of the released neutrons strike the bomb casing, which is made of Uranium-238 (the most abundant isotope of uranium), causing another fission explosion.

SOURCE: Adapted from an article in the *Encyclopedia Americana* by Dr. Edward Teller.

Opponents of H-bomb development, led by Oppenheimer, who was then chairman of the General Advisory Committee (GAC) to the AEC, argued that it would be immoral and unnecessary to produce a "weapon of this type whose power of destruction is essentially unlimited."[19] Others, such as Sen. McMahon, could see little moral difference between dropping one "superbomb" or several "small" atomic bombs on a civilian population, and their views prevailed.

The decisive breakthrough in the development of the hydrogen bomb, the development of a design idea by physicist Edward Teller and mathematician Stanislaw Ulam, came roughly a year after Truman's decision to build the bomb. The scheme the two scientists devised had something to do with how to configure a bomb so that a small atomic explosive would trigger a thermonuclear — or hydrogen — explosion. This invention laid to rest any doubts as to whether a usable hydrogen bomb could be built.

The United States tested its first H-bomb on Nov. 1, 1952, and its first "droppable" H-bomb in March 1954. The Soviet Union, despite the effort the United States had made to assure secrecy and loyalty, tested its first superbomb in November 1955. Whereas a little over four years had separated the first U.S. and Soviet A-bomb tests, only about a year and a half separated their first tests of droppable H-bombs.

In late 1953, President Eisenhower temporarily lifted Oppenheimer's security clearances because of allegations that the physicist was "disloyal" and "untrustworthy." The Atomic Energy Commission set up a special panel to hold hearings on the question. The motives for the investigation remain much in dispute. It is generally agreed, though, that Oppenheimer had made enemies for himself by opposing the hydrogen bomb and in arguing that U.S. military policy generally relied too much on atomic weapons.[20] Teller, father of the H-bomb, testified in May 1954 that Oppenheimer, father of the A-bomb, struck him as strange and untrustworthy. According to a scientist who knew both men well, Teller "wanted only to destroy Oppenheimer's political power, not to damage Oppenheimer himself."[21] However this may be, as a result of the investigation Oppenheimer permanently was stripped of his security clearances.

Consequences of 1954 Atomic Energy Act

As it happened, just the kinds of policies which Oppenheimer had opposed were coming into vogue with the Eisenhower administration. The administration advocated "massive retaliation," the doctrine that the United States should respond to

---

[19] Recommendations of GAC members to AEC, Oct. 30, 1949, reprinted in York, *op. cit.*, p. 157.

[20] See Harold P. Green, "The Oppenheimer Case: A Study in the Abuse of Law," *The Bulletin of the Atomic Scientists,* September 1977, pp. 12-61.

[21] Freeman Dyson, "Disturbing the Universe — III," *The New Yorker,* Aug. 20, 1979, p. 41. Dyson is a mathematian at the Institute for Advanced Study, Princeton, N.J.

any serious emergency with a threat to use nuclear weapons, and it introduced the "new look," which involved deployment of tactical nuclear weapons overseas. Both policies required some sharing of atomic information with allies, which now were more dependent than ever on the U.S. nuclear arsenal. This, together with high hopes for the peaceful uses of the atom, required revision of atomic energy legislation. The law that came about — the Atomic Energy Act of 1954 — was designed to liberalize access to restricted data. Ironically, it was the law under which an injunction was imposed on *The Progressive.*

The 1954 Atomic Energy Act, as it was described by the Joint Commitee on Atomic Energy, permitted the government to transfer to U.S. allies "data necessary to development of defense plans, the training of personnel . . . and the evaluation of the capabilities of potential enemies." But the new law "made clear that no information which would reveal important or significant data on the design or fabrication of the nuclear portions of atomic weapons, or on the detailed engineering of other important parts of atomic weapons, can be revealed."[22]

In the decade following passage of the 1954 Atomic Energy Act many countries began to acquire nuclear power plant technology. At the same time, nuclear weapons — including U.S. tactical weapons — were becoming more widely dispersed throughout the world. Britain, then France, and finally China tested their first atomic bombs, and then their first hydrogen bombs. With technology and information more widely disseminated, people began to warn that soon we would be living in a "world of nuclear powers." Such fears, and — at a more concrete level — anxiety that West Germany would be the next country to "go nuclear," contributed first to discussion and then negotiation of a treaty to prevent the spread of atomic weapons. The Non-Proliferation Treaty (NPT) was concluded in 1968.

The NPT was based on a tacit concession that the knowledge needed to build an atomic bomb was already, for all practical purposes, in the public domain. What the treaty attempted to do is control not atomic information but rather the materials needed to produce atomic bombs. This the treaty did by means of a system of "safeguards," monitoring and inspection procedures designed to detect in timely fashion the diversion of material from atomic power plants (and related facilities) to weapons production facilities. The treaty said nothing about hydrogen bombs as a special problem.

---

[22] Joint Committee on Atomic Energy, Senate Report No. 1699, *U.S. Code: Congressional and Administrative News* (1954), 83d Congress, 2nd Session, p. 3462.

Disputed Need for Atomic Secrecy

JIMMY Carter made a strong commitment during the 1976 presidential campaign to do more to curb nuclear proliferation, and as president he has attempted to address himself to the major criticisms that have been leveled at the Non-Proliferation Treaty. On the one hand, he has tried to persuade more countries to join the NPT, or at least to make explicit pledges to forego acquisition of atomic weapons. On the other hand, he has tried to curtail the dissemination of "sensitive technologies" which would be essential to bomb construction. These technologies include reprocessing plants, which could be used to extract plutonium from used atomic power plant fuel for use in weapons, and uranium enrichment facilities, which could be used to produce weapons-grade uranium. His administration has made no special effort, however, to curtail access to the information needed to make an atomic bomb, as this is generally conceded to be readily available. As for hydrogen bombs, up until the time *The Progressive* case broke, the administration apparently gave them no special attention as a proliferation problem.

Hydrogen bombs, in fact, have received remarkably little discussion in the literature on nuclear proliferation. Among six major studies of the nuclear proliferation problem which have appeared since 1974, none contains a chapter or paper devoted to the subject of thermonuclear explosives. Theodore B. Taylor, who more than any other individual has explored the types of equipment, technology, and expertise needed to build atomic bombs, makes no mention at all of hydrogen bombs as they are designed today in the book on nuclear safeguards that he wrote with Mason Willrich in 1974. The book contains a half-page discussion of "pure fusion" bombs — a type of hydrogen bomb, as yet undeveloped, which would require no fission-bomb trigger. But it concludes that this type of explosive probably could not be made any time in the foreseeable future "without highly sophisticated equipment and exceptionally highly skilled and experienced specialists."[23]

An Office of Technology Assessment study of nuclear proliferation which appeared in 1977 likewise makes no mention of hydrogen bombs. Of the remaining four studies, three mention H-bombs only in passing, and the fourth devotes just four pages to them. It concludes that a highly industrialized country such as Japan would be more likely to have an interest in H-bombs

---

[23] Mason Willrich and Theodore B. Taylor, *Nuclear Theft: Risks and Safeguards* (1974), p. 28.

than the kind of country which proliferation experts usually consider most likely to be next to "go nuclear."[24]

The lack of interest that students of proliferation have had in hydrogen bombs may reflect the view that once a country has acquired atomic bombs, the prerequisite for construction of a hydrogen bomb, the damage already is done. Once a country can kill several hundred thousand people with a single Hiroshima-style bomb, additional capabilities may be insignificant by comparison. While highly industrialized countries such as West Germany or Japan undoubtedly would want to build hydrogen bombs if they decided to go nuclear, countries like Pakistan, South Korea, South Africa, and Argentina might be quite content with the ability to demolish a few of their adversary's cities.

Lack of interest in hydrogen bombs also may reflect a view that the hydrogen bomb secret is a rapidly vanishing commodity, and that any attempt to prevent construction of hydrogen bombs once a country already has produced an atomic bomb is bound to fail. Since 1945, the time it has taken a country to test an H-bomb once it has tested an A-bomb has tended to decline, though France is an exception *(see box, p. 58).*

Administration's Position on H-Bombs

Carter administration officials insist that time is of the essence in countering nuclear proliferation. "It is of the highest and gravest importance to the United States that as few nations as possible develop thermonuclear weapons," Secretary of State Cyrus R. Vance said in his affidavit in *The Progressive* case. "We are committed to a policy of preventing the proliferation of these weapons." Publication of the Morland article, he continued, "would substantially increase the risk that thermonuclear weapons would become available or available at an earlier date to those who do not have them."[25]

Even if it now takes a country only a matter of years or months to build an H-bomb after building an A-bomb, administration officials argue, that is still time in which the international community can take action. They also say that even if the Teller-Ulam design ideas are much easier to figure out now that thousands of people have worked on H-bomb design and produc-

---

[24] *Nuclear Proliferation: Phase II*, eds. Robert M. Lawrence and Joel Larus (1974), p. 53. The other four studies mentioned are: U.S. Congress, Office of Technology Assessment, *Nuclear Proliferation and Safeguards* (1977); Stockholm International Peace Research Institute, *Nuclear Proliferation Problems* (1974); Onkar Marwah and Ann Schulz, eds., *Nuclear Proliferation and the Near-Nuclear Countries* (1975); The Annals of the American Academy of Political and Social Science, *Nuclear Proliferation: Prospects, Problems, and Proposals*, March 1977.

[25] Reprinted in *The Progressive*, May 1979, p. 36.

A-Bomb And H-Bomb Chronology

Nation	A-Bomb	H-Bomb	Difference (in years)
United States	1945	1952	7
Soviet Union	1949	1955	6
Britain	1952	1957	5
France	1960	1968	8
China	1964	1967	3

tion in at least five countries, the effort to make discovery of those ideas as hard as possible is still well worth the effort. Administration officials are reluctant to be quoted on matters that could affect the outcome of *The Progressive* case. But they stress that an H-bomb is much more powerful than an A-bomb. The radius of destruction caused by a typical H-bomb, for example, would be about ten times as great as that caused by a typical A-bomb.

Such arguments must be weighed against some more general considerations that frequently are mentioned by critics of atomic secrecy. First, the discovery of atomic energy has been the decisive factor in dividing what was once the world's most truly international community — the community of science — into competing national factions. Many people increasingly wonder whether the advantages of maintaining secrecy any longer justify the stifling effects secrecy has on free scientific inquiry. Second, atomic energy has had an exceptional status in that provisions for secrecy — including the right of prior restraint which the government claims in *The Progressive* case — ordinarily would be tolerated in the United States only in time of war. Third, to the extent America attempts to keep its atomic plans secret, and America's adversaries keep their secret, worst-case military planning tends to become inevitable on both sides. The assumption that the poorly understood adversary is doing the worst, critics of secrecy claim, has been an important factor speeding the arms race.

National Security Needs vs. Free Press

The complex issues raised by atomic secrecy are not the types of issues which U.S. courts like to have thrust on them. When weighty matters affecting the nation's security are at stake, and especially when extremely technical issues are involved, the courts would prefer to leave decisions to the executive branch or to the legislative process. In *The Progressive* case many believe the courts will be strongly predisposed to accept the government's views on what the national interest requires.

The strong presumption against any abridgment of a free press, however, introduces a volatile and unpredictable element into *The Progressive* case. Many analysts have compared the case to the 1971 Pentagon papers decision, in which the Supreme Court refused to grant the government an injunction against the publication of sensitive historic documents by *The New York Times*. But the Pentagon papers decision hardly provides a clear-cut guide to what the Supreme Court is likely to do about atomic secrecy.

Many analysts believe that the 1971 decision proves conclusively that *The Progressive* is bound to lose. The two justices who argued in 1971 that press freedom absolutely must not be abridged in any way under any circumstances, Justices Hugo L. Black and William O. Douglas, are no longer on the bench and have been replaced by persons who are much more sympathetic to the imperatives of national security. The other four justices who decided in favor of *The New York Times*[26] based their position in large part on the fact that Congress had enacted no statute authorizing prior restraint in the type of situation at issue. In the case of *The Progressive,* a statute which seems to provide for prior restraint of publication clearly exists. Moreover, *The Progressive* case involves information which could be of help to a future adversary, whereas the Pentagon papers involved history.

According to a contrary line of reasoning, the Pentagon papers case involved information which plainly had been classified and plainly had been stolen. *The Progressive* case involved information that had been declassified, albeit possibly by mistake. At the time *The New York Times* sought to publish the Pentagon papers, the United States was at war; today it is not. While the government may say now that the Pentagon papers were "just history," this is not what officials said in 1971. At that time they claimed that publication of the documents would do "grave and irreparable danger to the security of the United States."

If the courts decide to apply the "grave and irreparable danger" standard or something very much like it in *The Progressive* case, they may have difficulty defining exactly what the danger is. There is little in the literature on nuclear proliferation to indicate precisely how the spread of hydrogen bombs to countries that already have atomic bombs would gravely and irreparably jeopardize U.S. national security.

---

[26] Justices William J. Brennan Jr., Potter Stewart, Byron R. White and Thurgood Marshall.

Selected Bibliography

Books

Dyson, Freeman, *Disturbing the Universe,* Harper & Row, 1979.
Jungk, Robert, *Brighter Than a Thousand Suns,* Harcourt, Brace and Co., 1958.
Lapp, Ralph E., *The New Priesthood,* Harper & Row, 1965.
York, Herbert, *The Advisors: Oppenheimer, Teller and the Superbomb,* W. H. Freeman and Company, 1976.

Articles

Day, Samuel H. Jr., "The Nuclear Weapons Labs," *The Bulletin of the Atomic Scientists,* April 1977.
———"The Nicest People Make the Bomb," *The Progressive,* October 1978.
Feld, Bernard T., "The Progressive Secret," *The Bulletin of the Atomic Scientists,* May 1979.
Hentoff, Nat, articles in *Inquiry,* May 14, 1979, June 11, 1979, and June 25, 1979; and in *Village Voice,* April 16, 1979, April 23, 1979, April 30, 1979, and May 7, 1979.
Morland, Howard, "Tritium: The New Genie," *The Progressive,* February 1979.
The Progressive, May 1979, entire issue.

Reports and Studies

Editorial Research Reports, "First Amendment and Mass Media," 1970 Vol. I, p. 41; "Nuclear Proliferation," 1978 Vol. I, p. 201; and "Secrecy in Government," 1971 Vol. II, p. 627.
Holloway, David, "Entering the Nuclear Arms Race: The Soviet Decision to Build the Atomic Bomb, 1939-45," International Security Studies Program, The Wilson Center, Working Paper No. 9, Washington, D.C., 1979.
Mark, J. Carson, "A Short Account of Los Alamos Theoretical Work on Thermonuclear Weapons, 1946-1950," U.S. Atomic Energy Commission, July 1974.
"Publishing, Perishing, and the First Amendment," Alicia Patterson Foundation Conference on *The Progressive* Case, New York City, April 17, 1979.
"Report of the Defense Science Board: Task Force on Secrecy," Office of the Director of Defense Research and Engineering, Washington, D.C., July 1, 1970.

D ETERMINING
RADIATION DANGERS

by

William Sweet

Aug. 10
1 9 7 9

(**Report update:** Since August 1979, a continuing controversy about radiation dangers has led to a number of changes in regulations and recommended standards. In December 1979, the Environmental Protection AGency lowered the standard for exposure of the public to radiation from normal nuclear reactor operations 20-fold, from 500 millirem/year to 25 millirem/year.

Government agencies now are debating whether to adopt changes for occupational exposure which the International Commission on Radiological Protection recommended in 1977. EPA favors the general thrust of "ICRP 26," which suggested separate standards for exposure to internal and external sources of radiation, but the Nuclear Regulatory Commission opposes adoption of ICRP 26 because the recommended standard for internal radiation amounts to a relaxation rather than a tightening of existing regulations.

During the past year, the "BEIR III" committee of the National Academy of Sciences has remained unable to resolve its differnces about low-level radiation [see p. 75]. Its final report, which is to be published in the summer of 1980, is expected to contain two dissenting minority positions — one arguing that the consensus recommendation overstates radiation dangers, the other arguing that it understates them.)

DETERMINING RADIATION DANGERS

MORE than half a century has elapsed since women laced their eye shadow with radium to make their eyelids glow, and today any educated person would regard such a practice with horrified condescension. Yet 50 years from now, if some experts are to be believed, the routine diagnostic X-ray may be seen — like radioactive mascara — as the barbaric custom of a bygone era. According to these experts, accumulating evidence suggests radiation is much more dangerous at low levels of exposure than generally appreciated, and the U.S. government therefore should lose no time in tightening standards.

Other equally reputable experts remain convinced that low-level radiation poses a negligible health hazard, and these experts advocate retention of current standards. At stake in the growing controversy over low-level radiation are not only widespread medical practices but also certain military doctrines and, above all else, the future of the nuclear power industry.

Most of the studies on which radiation critics rely involve complex methodologies and produce ambiguous results. What gives the critics strong credibility with the public is not so much the studies as a large number of incidents which seem to call the vigilance of authorities into question. The accident at the Three Mile Island nuclear power plant near Harrisburg, Pa., made a particularly strong impact on public perceptions. Extensive press and television coverage in the days following the March 28 accident made tens of millions of Americans more fully alert to the danger that escaping radiation holds for large populations.

According to a staff report submitted to the Nuclear Regulatory Commission on Aug. 2, some radioactivity was released into the atmosphere at Three Mile Island but the staff found nothing to alter the conclusion of several investigative agencies in May that the radiation posed only "minimal risks" to the people who lived nearby. However, the report did say that emissions of some radioactive gases were 11 times above recommended levels. Other official reports are still awaited. Whatever their findings may be, it is clear that Three Mile Island has combined with other incidents in recent years to undermine confidence in radiation protection.

Unguarded radium dumps dating from the 1920s and 1930s have been discovered in Colorado and New Jersey. Concern has mounted about the safety of people who were allowed to build homes with radioactive wastes from uranium and phosphate mines during the 1950s. The regional director of the federal Environmental Protection Agency's radiation programs in Denver announced recently that water supplies in hundreds of communities in 15 western states may be dangerously contaminated with low-level radiation from uranium mines and mills.

Congressional hearings have publicized charges that the government ignored and concealed evidence that atomic bomb tests in Nevada during the 1950s and early 1960s caused leukemia and other cancers among people living in the tri-state area around St. George, Utah.[1] Experts from the Departments of Interior, Energy and Defense have had trouble deciding whether test sites in the South Pacific now are safe for human habitation, and as a result natives of Bikini were moved back to their home in this decade only to be ordered out again in 1978.

With increasing numbers of people starting to suspect that they may have contracted cancer as a result of exposure to radiation, claims for compensation are piling up with the government and in court. Residents of Red Rock, N.M., where lung cancer rates have soared among Navajo uranium miners, have sought compensation from the government since 1971. Stewart L. Udall, the former Secretary of the Interior, and fellow attorney Dale Haralson represent more than 600 clients in Arizona, Utah and Nevada in filing claims connected with some 400 deceased people who were exposed to fallout.[2]

---

[1] Joint hearings on health effects of fallout, held in April 1979, by the Senate Subcommittee on Health & Scientific Research, under the chairmanship of Sen. Edward M. Kennedy, D-Mass., and the House Subcommittee on Oversight and Investigations, under Rep. Bob Eckhardt, D-Texas.

[2] A recent study reported a 2.4% higher rate of leukemia mortality in a group exposed to high levels of radiation in the high fallout counties of Utah; for unexplained reasons leukemia mortality among people exposed to little radiation was about half the national average. Joseph L. Lyon, et al., "Childhood Leukemias Associated with Fallout from Nuclear Testing," *The New England Journal of Medicine*, Feb. 22, 1979, pp. 397-402.

An Oklahoma City jury in May awarded $10.5 million in damages to relatives of Karen Silkwood, a worker and union organizer at a Kerr-McGee Corp. fuel-fabrication plant near Oklahoma City, who somehow became contaminated with plutonium and subsequently died in an auto crash under strange circumstances. The jury found Kerr-McGee responsible for Silkwood's contamination, rejecting the company's claim that she might have contaminated herself. In a significant ruling, the judge held that a company may be held liable for damages even if it has met government radiation standards. The verdict, if upheld in higher courts, could result in billions of dollars worth of suits being filed against the government, the nuclear industry and the medical profession.

Types and Biological Effects of Radiation

The kind of radiation of concern in the debate over health hazards is called "ionizing radiation," that is, electrically charged radiation which ruptures the chemical bonds that join atoms together in molecules.[3] Ionizing radiation which passes through biological tissue can prevent a cell from dividing, or it can damage the genetic material contained in the cell's nucleus, causing it to divide abnormally. Harmful effects can be "somatic," which show up in damage to the individual organism, or genetic — mutations which show up only in future generations.

There are five kinds of ionizing radiation of biological significance: alpha particles, beta particles, gamma rays, neutrons, and X-rays. Though primarily artificial, in the human environment, X-rays also enter the atmosphere as part of cosmic radiation. The other forms of radiation are emitted by radioactive substances such as radium, uranium and thorium.

Any radioactive element decays at a characteristic rate called its "half life," which defines the period in which the element loses one-half of its radioactivity. The longer the "half life," the less intense is the radioactivity. Elements which have short half lives accordingly emit radiation at a very intense rate, but they also become biologically harmless more rapidly.

The forms of ionizing radiation emitted in the process of radioactive decay are classified as low or high "linear energy transfer" (LET). The heavy particles — neutrons and alpha particles — are high LET. Their penetrating power is weak because they quickly transfer energy to other substances. But if they do enter an organism, by inhalation, ingestion, or through an abrasion, they emit a dense trail of ionization and are intensely harmful. Beta particles and gamma rays, classified as

---

[3] Non-ionizing radiation, such as ultra-violet light and radiation emitted by microwave ovens and high-powered radar, also may be harmful, but it generally is treated as a separate subject because of its distinct physical properties, sources and biological effects.

low LET, are less intensely harmful but are much more penetrating.

The absorption of radiation by other substances is measured in rads, a precise physical quantity defined as the amount of radiation that will cause one kilogram (2.2 pounds) of material to absorb 0.01 joules of energy. Different kinds of radiation do different amounts of damage to living tissue at any given level of exposure; exposure to one rad of beta radiation, in other words, is not precisely as harmful as exposure to one rad of alpha radiation. The rad therefore is adjusted by a measure of biological effectiveness called the "quality factor"; the factor is one for beta and gamma radiation, and roughly 10 to 20 for neutrons and alpha particles. Multiplication of the dose absorbed by the quality factor yields the "dose equivalent," expressed in rems, the standard measure of biological impact. Since the rem is a large quantity, human exposure to radiation generally is expressed in millirems. One millirem is one-thousandth of a rem.

However, even millirems provide only the crudest estimate of how radiation affects tissue. Rapidly dividing cells, such as are found in the human fetus, are exceptionally vulnerable. Radiation is more harmful to women than to men, and some age groups are unusually susceptible to certain kinds of cancer. Young children, for example, are especially vulnerable to leukemia. Certain radioactive elements, moreover, tend to concentrate in specific parts of the body, where they can emit harmful radiation over a longer period of time. Strontium-90 migrates to the bones; plutonium concentrates in the liver and in the bones, and secondarily in human gonads. Many radioactive substances enter the food chain on which both animals and humans depend.[4]

Sources of Radiation: Natural and Artificial

Most radiation to which humans are exposed comes from natural sources *(see table, p. 67).* Cosmic rays account for about one-third of the natural background radiation on average — more in high altitudes and less closer to sea-level — and terrestrial sources for close to one-half. A building material such as granite contains small amounts of radioactive materials and emits appreciable amounts of radiation. In a few parts of the world — the southern Indian state of Kerela is a notable example — deposits of radioactive materials are so large that they are thought to explain exceptionally high rates of genetic defects such as mental retardation.

---

[4] For a fuller treatment of radiation and its health effects, see Chapter 2 of *Nuclear Power and the Environment* (1976) by the (British) Royal Commission on Environmental Pollution, and Chapter 5 of *Nuclear Power: Issues and Choices* (1977) by the (Ford Foundation's) Nuclear Energy Policy Study Group.

Estimates of Annual Radiation Dosage
Per Person in the United States

Source of Radiation	Average Dose Rate (in millirems)	Source of Radiation	Average Dose Rate (in millirems)
Natural		*Artificial*	
Environmental		Environmental	
cosmic	45	Global fallout	4
		Nuclear power	0.003
Terrestrial	60	Medical	73
Internal radio-		Occupational	0.8
active isotopes	25	Miscellaneous	2
Total	130	Total	80

Source: Compiled from official sources by the (Ford Foundation's) Nuclear Energy Policy Group for the year 1970 and published in its 1977 report *Nuclear Power: Issues and Choices*, p. 163.

Among the sources of radiation not ordinarily found in nature, X-rays account for overwhelmingly the largest portion of average human exposure, while radionuclides used in medical diagnosis and therapy make a small but noticeable contribution. A typical chest X-ray series can expose the patient to roughly 250 millirems — more than the total radiation dose a U.S. resident ordinarily receives in a year. In 1978 about 162 million diagnostic X-rays were administered for medical purposes and 86 million for dental purposes; radionuclides were administered in close to 8 million cases.[5]

Many leading health physicists believe that current levels of exposure to X-rays are unwarranted by any standard and could be sharply reduced without detriment to medical practices. Dr. Karl Z. Morgan, who often is referred to as the father of health physics in the United States, has argued that the dose delivered by medical diagnostic X-rays could be reduced by 90 percent, while at the same time increasing the quality and amount of diagnostic information available.[6] The licensing of X-ray technicians is required by only 10 states: Arizona, California, Delaware, Hawaii, Kentucky, Montana, New Jersey, New York, Oregon and West Virginia.

The Public Health Service, the American College of Radiology and the American College of Chest Physicians in 1972 all recommended against using chest X-rays for routine tuberculosis

---

[5] According to Bureau of Radiological Health estimates.

[6] Karl Z. Morgan, "Cancer and Low Level Ionizing Radiation," *The Bulletin of the Atomic Scientists*, September 1978, p. 39. See also Herbert L. Abrams, "The 'Overutilization' of X-rays," *The New England Journal of Medicine*, May 24, 1979, pp. 1213-1216.

screening, and the federal Food and Drug Administration — in cooperation with the National Cancer Institute — now operates a program urging doctors and hospitals to reduce unnecessary radiation exposure in mammography. Under new guidelines, issued at the recommendation of a special task force headed by the Environmental Protection Agency, dental X-rays are not to be given as part of a routine screening test in government hospitals. While still further restrictions may follow, X-rays will continue to be used, albeit more sparingly. They provide medical information that cannot otherwise be obtained.

The situation is quite different with regard to the two other main artificial sources of radiation, nuclear weapon testing and the nuclear power industry. Concern about fallout was the single most important factor in generating pressure for an atmospheric test ban treaty in 1963 (*see p. 74*), and it helped persuade France to stop its atmospheric testing in the mid-1970s. Today only China continues to conduct atmospheric tests.

The nuclear power industry, on the other hand, could be profoundly affected by the controversy. Today nuclear power accounts for less than one millirem of the average American's annual exposure to radiation, seemingly a trivial amount. The level of exposure would rise with expansion of nuclear power.

Focus on Hazards in the Nuclear Industry

Even critics of the nuclear industry usually concede that the public is exposed to relatively little radiation as a result of ordinary reactor operations.[7] It is generally agreed that releases of effluent gases such as iodine, xenon and krypton isotopes and of carbon-14 at current levels pose little danger to public health. Catastrophic reactor accidents are another matter. The most exhaustive study of accident scenarios theorizes that the worst accident possible would cause 3,300 fatalities and some 45,000 cases of radiation sickness, and it reckoned the chances of such an accident occurring at one in 200 million.[8]

The probability of catastrophic accident remains in dispute, however, and estimates of health effects are sensitive to the impact assigned low-level radiation. A secret study done for the Atomic Energy Commission by Brookhaven National Laboratory is said to have concluded in 1964-65 that a major accident

---

[7] An exception is Dr. Ernest J. Sternglass, who claims that reactors emit strontium-90 and pose a much greater risk to public health than generally thought. See, for example, his presentation to the Second Congressional Seminar on Low-Level Ionizing Radiation, "Cancer Mortality Changes Around Nuclear Facilities in Connecticut," in the seminar's published proceedings *Radiation Standards and Public Health* (1978), pp. 174-212.

[8] WASH-1400, generally known as the Rasmussen Report, for its principal author, Dr. Norman Rasmussen, a professor of nuclear engineering at the Massachusetts Institute of Technology. Cited in *Nuclear Power: Issues and Choices*, p. 178.

Military Implications of the Radiation Debate

Estimates of casualties that would result from either a "limited" or an "all-out" nuclear war are highly speculative, since numerous important variables — such as the targeting strategies selected by the governments at war and the climatic conditions at the time of war — cannot be predicted. All casualty estimates would have to be raised, however, if low-level radiation turns out to be more dangerous than previously thought.

If the most severe critics of radiation standards are right, Professor Henry Kendall of the Massachusetts Institute of Technology calculates that an all-out nuclear war could result in hundreds of millions of cancers worldwide rather than tens of millions. On the most pessimistic estimates, one billion people or roughly a quarter of the world's population might contract cancer as a result of nuclear war, in addition to the one billion who would fall prey to cancer anyway.

might create an "area of disaster . . . equal to that of the state of Pennsylvania."[9]

Under ordinary conditions, most people agree, the preparation and disposal of reactor fuel pose greater risks to public health than do reactor operations. The disposal of spent — used — reactor fuel, some of which remains highly radioactive for hundreds of thousands of years, involves technical problems that have not been solved. If radioactive materials escape from a disposal site, they might contaminate the atmosphere or groundwater over a wide area.[10]

Not only the "back end" waste disposal but also the front end of the nuclear fuel cycle presents unresolved problems. In the course of mining and milling uranium, radon and decay products called "radon daughters" are released, and these emit alpha particles which can cause cancer if they lodge in the lungs. Respiratory cancer rates have soared among people who mined

[9] Quoted by Daniel F. Ford and Henry W. Kendall, "Catastrophic Nuclear Reactor Accidents," in *The Nuclear Fuel Cycle* (1975), p. 80.

[10] For background, see "Nuclear Waste Disposal," *E.R.R.*, 1976 Vol. II, pp. 883-906.

uranium during the 1940s and 1950s.[11] And while the industry claims that this particular problem has now been solved by means of proper ventilation, the disposal of mill tailings — waste products left after extraction of uranium from ore — presents many problems that have yet to be adequately explored.[12] Even though the radiation released by the tailing at any given time is small, the cumulative hazards associated with that form of radiation may be greater than has been assumed. Over a period of 100,000 years, the cumulative radiation from the tailings becomes "the dominant contribution to radiation exposure from the nuclear fuel cycle."[13]

Fears Over Reprocessing and 'Fast Breeders'

Reprocessing and recycling of spent reactor fuels, procedures in which plutonium and uranium are extracted to be re-used as new fuel, could significantly increase human exposure to low-level radiation. Fuel obtained by means of reprocessing could be used either in conventional reactors or, someday, in "fast breeders," reactors awaiting commercial use that produce more new fuel than they consume. However, the reprocessing would liberate gaseous and volatile radio-isotopes.[14]

Recycling of plutonium, especially if commercial fast-breeder reactors were built, would introduce an important new source of high-LET radiation into the nuclear fuel cycle. Critics of nuclear energy often point out that a ball of plutonium the size of an orange could give every person alive on earth lung cancer if particles were distributed to everybody.

On the other hand, a defender of nuclear energy, Dr. Ralph Lapp, maintains that this kind of comparison is as senseless as it would be "to assert that a single adult's sperm is sufficient to impregnate every female on earth."[15] For now the issue is moot; the Carter administration has suspended commercial reprocessing in the United States and has discouraged the introduction of breeder reactors.[16] But many other countries plan to deploy commercial reprocessing facilities and breeder reactors, and there is industry pressure in the United States to do the same.

Excluding reprocessing and recycling operations and catastrophic accidents, the hazards to public health posed by reactor

---

[11] See Arell S. Schurgin and Thomas C. Hollacher's "Radiation Induced Lung Cancers Among Uranium Miners," in *The Nuclear Fuel Cycle,* pp. 9-46, and H. Peter Metzger's *The Atomic Establishment* (1972), pp. 115-144.

[12] See *Report to the President by the Inter-agency Review Group on Nuclear Waste Management,* TID-28817 (draft), DIST. Category UC-70, October 1978, p. xiv.

[13] Victor Gilinsky, presentation at the Pacific Southwest Minerals and Energy Conference, Anaheim, Calif., May 2, 1978, Nuclear Regulatory Commission, Office of Public Affairs, No. S-78-3, p. 3.

[14] *Nuclear Power: Issues and Choices,* p. 182.

[15] Ralph E. Lapp, *The Radiation Controversy* (1979), p. 123.

[16] The administration has been motivated primarily by concern that the spread of reprocessing plants would accelerate the proliferation of atomic weapons, not by anxiety about the toxic effects of plutonium. See "Nuclear Proliferation," *E.R.R.,* 1978 Vol. I, pp. 201-220.

operations are widely thought to compare favorably with coal, and even with the newest and cleanest coal technologies.[17] Hazards to workers in the nuclear industry are more controversial. Dr. Bernard L. Cohen, a prominent defender of nuclear power, claims that the occupational risk of cancer in the nuclear industry would result in a loss of life expectancy of about 20 days, far less than the toll of occupational accidents (79 days) among all U.S. workers.[18]

Government statistics on workers in nuclear power plants indicate that in 1977 only 270 out of 71,904 were exposed to more than five rems, the Nuclear Regulatory Commission's "maximum permissible" level for occupational exposure *(see p. 74)*. Critics contend, however, that these seemingly favorable results are achieved only by employing many workers on very short assignments under intense exposure. Moreover, it is argued that the five-rem limit on occupational exposure is itself much too high. This claim is at the heart of the controversy over low-level radiation, for many people think a lower limit would spell the end of nuclear power in America.

Evolution of Exposure Standards

T HE CURRENT limits on public and occupational exposure are only the latest of several radiation standards, which have been revised repeatedly as health effects have become better understood. When radiation first was discovered, the excitement of uncovering a heretofore unknown world far outweighed any thought of detrimental biological effects. Wilhelm Conrad Röntgen's discovery of X-rays in 1895 and Henry Becquerel's finding in 1896 that uranium spontaneously emits radiation ushered in one of the great eras of science.[19]

Scientists were quick to learn that radiation in large doses could cause skin lesions, and some early experimentalists burned themselves intentionally with radioactive substances in order to study their biological effects first-hand. But the most detrimental effects appeared only in time when the early experimenters fell prey to cancer. Marie Curie was but one of many such victims, who probably numbered in the hundreds, but hers certainly made the most dramatic story.

It was Marie Curie who had done most of the experimental work in refining radioactive substances like polonium and ra-

[17] *Nuclear Power: Issues and Choices,* p. 196. See also "America's Coal Economy," *E.R.R.*, 1978 Vol. I, pp. 281-300.
[18] Bernard L. Cohen, "What Is the Misunderstanding All About?" *The Bulletin of the Atomic Scientists,* Feb. 1979, p. 53.
[19] See George Lindenberg Clark's "X-Rays," *Encyclopaedia Britannica* (1973), Vol. 23, p. 846.

dium, which she discovered, while her husband Pierre Curie concentrated on studying their properties and on theoretical matters. As a result of her work, Marie Curie shared Nobel Prizes in 1903 (with Becquerel and with Pierre) and in 1911 (with Pierre) but died of leukemia in 1934. In a remarkably symmetrical twist of fate, her daughter Irène also married one of the great physicists of the age (Frédéric Joliot-Curie), discovered with him in 1934 that radioactive substances could be produced artifically, shared a Nobel Prize with him in 1935, and died of leukemia in 1956.

By the time of Irène Joliot-Curie's death the carcinogenic properties of radiation were well known, and the need for radiological protection was well established. The American Roentgen Ray Society had published recommendations for X-ray protection as early as 1921, and 1925 saw the creation of the International Commission on Radiological Protection (ICRP), an independent group of radiation health scientists — currently 12 — which is answerable to the world's professional radiologists meeting in congress. The ICRP adopted recommendations that occupational exposure be limited to 0.2 roentgen per day in 1934, and this was the standard for most nations until 1950.

Studies of Japanese Atom Bomb Survivors

The atomic bombing of Hiroshima and Nagasaki exposed for the first time big populations to the lingering effects of radiation. Of some 350,000 people in Hiroshima at the time of the blast, 140,000 had died by the end of 1945, according to the best available estimates; in Nagasaki roughly 74,000 out of 280,000 died.[20] The survivors provided the raw material for the first large-scale study of the biological effects of exposure to varying levels of radiation.

Collection of data and materials at Hiroshima and Nagasaki began in 1945 and was consolidated in 1947 under the aegis of the U.S.-created Atomic Bomb Casualty Commission. Most survivors were interviewed, and special bomb tests were arranged in Nevada to simulate conditions in Hiroshima and Nagasaki at the time of the blasts, as a means of estimating exposure levels in different parts of the two cities. Thousands of items — photographs, pathological specimens and dissection records — were collected. Some 82,000 survivors were selected for a Life Span Study and 26,000 others made up a control group matched for age and sex. In 1973 many of the materials collected by the Casualty Commission were returned to Japan, at the behest of Japanese scientists, and in 1975 the commission was replaced by the Radiation Effects Research Foundation, which is managed jointly by Japan and the United States.

[20] Figures cited by Frank Barnaby, "The Continuing Body Count at Hiroshima and Nagasaki," *The Bulletin of the Atomic Scientists,* December 1977, p. 51.

The results of the Hiroshima-Nagasaki research, as summarized by the Natural Science Group — a body organized by the Geneva-based International Peace Bureau to appraise the Japanese studies — were in some ways predictable and in some ways surprising. The incidence of leukemia among survivors increased fast for a decade, peaking at a level 30 times the normal Japanese rate. Thyroid, breast and lung cancers appeared at significantly higher-than-normal rates among those exposed to initial radiation in both cities. Malignant tumors — salivary gland tumors, gastric carcinoma, bone tumors, prostate cancer, malignant lymphoma, etc. — appeared at an abnormally high rate after an average latency period of about 20 years.

However, death rates from non-malignant causes have been lower than average among survivors. While children exposed in the womb suffered an increase in birth defects, they have not proved to be more susceptible to leukemia than other Japanese children. Most startling of all, even though it has been established since 1927 that radiation causes genetic mutations, no significant genetic effects have been found in the survivor population.[21]

Paradoxically, the absence of certain expected effects such as genetic damage has suggested to some experts that radiation in low amounts may be more dangerous — not less dangerous — than previously thought. Dr. Joseph Rotblat, former president of the British Institute of Radiology, has argued that the bomb survivors "may be a selected population" in which "only the genetically toughest individuals survived the injuries and trauma" of nuclear attack. "Whether this hypothesis is valid or not, the evidence . . . strongly suggests that these survivors are in a special category. They may not be suitable as the basis for calculating radiation risk factors for other populations."[22]

People who entered the cities after the atomic explosions may provide a better basis for calculating health hazards from low-level radiation. Studies of some 40,000 Japanese who went to look for friends and relatives suggest a high incidence of radiation-related cancer, according to a recent report from Dr. Alice Stewart, a leading British radiologist.[23] Norman Solomon, a free-lance writer, has reported that U.S. soldiers who performed clean-up duties in the two cities show "many confirmed cases of leukemia, other unusual blood diseases, and bone marrow cancers."[24] Survivor studies have been criticized on the ground that

---

[21] "The Physical and Medical Effects of the Hiroshima and Nagasaki Bombs," *The Bulletin of the Atomic Scientists,* December 1977, pp. 54-56.

[22] J. Rotblat, "The Risks for Radiation Workers," *The Bulletin of the Atomic Scientists,* September 1978, p. 44.

[23] Cited in *The Washington Post,* Feb. 18, 1978.

[24] Norman Solomon, "Nagasaki's Other Victims," *The Progressive,* July 1979, p. 21.

much of the information collected is not open to public scrutiny. The Casualty Commission classified all of its data, and during the years immediately after World War II, U.S. occupation forces in Japan "censored all articles about the A-bombs."[25]

Bomb Test Fallout; 'Tolerance Dose' Levels

During the first decade that the Atomic Bomb Casualty Commission was collecting materials and data, sizable new groups of people were being exposed regularly to radiation for the first time: workers in the nuclear weapons production industry, people connected with the U.S. Navy's nuclear submarine program, and people exposed to fallout from weapons testing. Very little was known during this period about the direct effects of radioactive substances on humans, and the situation of employees in the nuclear weapons industry — most of whom did highly secret work at remote installations — received scant attention.

A radiation "tolerance dose" of 0.3 rem per week, equivalent to 15 rem per year, was set in 1949. In 1954-55, H. J. Muller — one of the leading radiation geneticists of the time — published research suggesting that low-level radiation has stronger genetic effects than was previously realized. Dr. Stewart reported in 1956 on damage to human fetuses from pre-natal X-rays. The same year, an international outcry over nuclear weapons testing was reaching a peak, and Democratic presidential candidate Adlai E. Stevenson was making a call for a test ban an important part of his campaign. An especially potent element in the struggle against testing was the presence of strontium-90 in the fallout. It concentrates in milk and therefore poses a particularly grave threat to the health of small children.

Largely in response to the growing outcry, President Eisenhower authorized test ban negotiations with the Soviet Union, and in 1959 he established the Federal Radiation Council to advise him on "radiation matters directly or indirectly affecting health." In 1960, the occupational tolerance dose was lowered roughly threefold to five rem per year, at the recommendation of the ICRP, and the standard for the public was set at 0.5 rem per year — one-tenth of the occupational dose. The term "tolerance dose" was changed to "permissible dose" in 1964 in an effort to stress that any exposure to radiation may be harmful. Most important of all, in 1963 the United States, the Soviet Union and Britain agreed to the atmospheric test-ban treaty.

As an arms control measure, the test ban has been much criticized, primarily because the superpowers accelerated underground testing after 1963,[26] but as an environmental protection

---

[25] Barnaby, *op. cit.*, p. 50.
[26] See "Politics of Strategic Arms Negotiations," *E.R.R.*, 1977 Vol. I, pp. 249-272.

measure the treaty achieved its purpose. Fallout lessened and so did public concern about radiation. The Nixon administration abolished the Federal Radiation Council in 1970 and transferred its responsibilities to the Environmental Protection Agency.

EPA's radiation record has come under increasingly heavy fire. The only radiation standard the agency has set since 1970, a 25 millirem ceiling on exposure of the general public to emissions from the nuclear fuel cycle, has not been enforced, according to Robert Alvarez, a radiation expert with the Environmental Policy Center in Washington, D.C.[27] Critics such as Alvarez say the agency has allowed authority over radiation standards to slip away, in fact if not in name, to the Department of Energy and the Nuclear Regulatory Commission (NRC), which sometimes are accused of being allied with the nuclear industry. On the other hand, defenders of current standards point out that NRC guidelines requiring protective measures could require the nuclear industry to spend vast sums if some assumptions about the health effects of low-level radiation are borne out.[28]

Several special panels have tried to resolve the life-or-death issue of low-level radiation on the basis of determining the best research results and by means of reasoned discussions. The two most important panels have been the Advisory Committee on the Biological Effects of Ionizing Radiation (the BEIR committee), established by the National Academy of Sciences and now at work on its third report since 1972, and a Radiation Inter-Agency Task Force which President Carter set up. But these panels have been unable to reach agreement on the key policy issues or even reach consensus about what is and what is not scientifically proven.

Scientific Basis for Controversy

T HE CONTROVERSY over low-level radiation revolves around the relationship of biological effects to radiation doses at low ranges of exposure. Under the "threshold" hypothesis, the potential danger of radiation drops sharply at low levels of exposure. It is assumed that human cells generally must incur radiation damage more than one time before serious biological effects show up, and that in most cases cell damage is repaired before the critical threshold is reached. The "threshold" theorists frequently argue that the human species has adjusted to radiation at levels approximating those found in nature, and

---

[27] Interview, July 16, 1979.
[28] For calculations of additional spending to reduce cancer risks, see Lapp, *op. cit.*, p. 76, and Morgan, *op. cit.*, p. 39.

that small added increments to natural background radiation make little difference.

Others contend that radiation is harmful in some degree at any level whatsoever. Proponents of what probably is the most widely accepted hypothesis, the "linear" theory, believe that biological effects are directly proportional to doses at all levels of exposure.[29] Some scientists take an even more cautious view of radiation dangers, and argue that more biological effects may occur per unit of radiation dose at low levels of exposure than at high levels. At high levels, according to this reasoning, many cells are killed outright and no further damage occurs.

Experts disagree about which of the three theories is correct not only for radiation in general but also for each kind of radiation. Some experts think, for example, that the relationship between dose and effect is super-linear for high-LET radiation (alpha particles and neutrons), while the threshold theory correctly describes low-LET radiation such as X-rays and gamma rays. The BEIR committee, in a preliminary report (BEIR III) issued May 2, argued in guarded terms for the linear theory: ". . .[I]n most cases the linear hypothesis emerged by default as . . . least objectionable. . . ."[30]

A majority of the committee estimated the risk from low-level ionizing radiation "in the range of 70 to 353 excess cases of fatal cancer per million persons per rad per year for single exposure."[31] A minority of the committee argued in a written dissent, however, that the risk estimates were too high. So deep was the split between the two factions that the preliminary report in May now has been withdrawn, and so volatile is opinion on the issue of low-level radiation that the minority faction in May now is said to be a majority.

Disputed Studies About Incidence of Cancer

Individual estimates of excess cancers caused by low-level radiation are reported to vary among members of the committee from 10 per million persons per rad per year to 1,000 per million per rad per year.[32] Even at the higher end of this range, experts stress biological effects would be very rare and detectable only in very large populations. Since the precise biological mechanism by means of which radiation causes cancer is unknown, the existence and magnitude of health effects can be demonstrated only in meticulous statistical studies, which must be controlled for many complicating factors such as age and sex.

---

[29] A directly proportional relationship between two variables is put in graph form as a straight line; hence the "linear" theory.

[30] Quoted in Committee on the Biological Effects of Ionizing Radiation, "The Effects on Populations of Exposure to Low Levels of Ionizing Radiation," p. 239.

[31] National Research Council, "BEIR Committee Issues New Estimates of Radiation Risks," press release, May 2, 1979. This release subsequently was withdrawn for revision.

[32] Interview with Howard J. Lewis, public affairs officer with the National Research Council, July 20, 1979.

Who's in Charge?

"...[T]he most important, most influential and universally applied standards are not laws or regulations, or even codes of practice. They are simply recommendations of the International Commission on Radiological Protection, the National Council on Radiation Protection and Measurements, and publications of the National Academy of Sciences, the national research councils such as the BEIR report.

"There are many government agencies which get into the act of setting, interpreting and enforcing radiation protection standards, and this is part of the problem.... First, exposure in uranium mines. We have the Bureau of Mines, the Labor Department, the Nuclear Regulatory Commission, the Public Health Service, the Department of Energy (DOE), the Environmental Protection Agency, and the state agencies....

"Or the permanent disposal of radioactive wastes: EPA, Department of Agriculture, DOE, Department of Transportation, NRC, ICC [Interstate Commerce Commission], state agencies...."

—Dr. Karl Z. Morgan,
Second Congressional Seminar on Low-Level
Ionizing Radiation, Feb. 10, 1978

Because radioactive substances came into widespread use only a generation ago, and because the latency period for most cancers is quite long, there are few groups of people suitable for study. Moreover, the few groups that have been studied frequently turn up unexpected and seemingly bizarre results — such as the lack of genetic effects in the Hiroshima-Nagasaki studies — which cast doubt on the methodology used or the suitability of the people selected.

The work which has been of decisive importance in the radiation controversy includes surveys done by Dr. Stewart and Dr. George Kneale in Britain and by Dr. Irwin Bross in the United States on pre-natal (in utero) induction of cancer by diagnostic X-rays; Dr. Thomas Najarian's study of nuclear submarine workers at the Portsmouth, N.H., shipyard; and a study of workers at the Hanford (Wash.) Nuclear Reservation by Dr. Thomas Mancuso, in cooperation with Stewart and Kneale (the "MSK" study). As summarized by Dr. Morgan, the Bross study showed a "5,000 percent increased risk of cancer among the children who had been exposed to diagnostic X-ray in utero, and who later developed certain respiratory diseases," while Najarian "reported a 450 percent higher death rate from leukemia among the radiation workers than the general population."[33] The Mancuso study, probably the most important and

---

[33] Karl Z. Morgan, *op. cit.*, p. 30 and p. 32.

definitely the most controversial of all, found a very small but statistically significant increase in radiation-related deaths at levels of exposure so low that most experts would have expected no significant effect.

Dr. Mancuso's study has caused a furor not only because of its surprising results but also because of the manner in which government agencies handled his contract. In 1977, just when he was beginning to produce results, the Energy Research and Development Administration (ERDA) relieved him of his research contract and transferred the work to government employees at Oak Ridge, Tenn.

Documents released to Mancuso under the Freedom of Information Act indicated that the Atomic Energy Commission originally commissioned him to do a study in order to fend off worker compensation claims, and that ERDA terminated his contract because he refused to contradict research indicating low-level radiation had affected the health of Hanford employees. Reporting on disclosures brought out in hearings conducted by Rep. Paul G. Rogers, D-Fla., in February 1978, *Science* magazine observed that the transfer of Mancuso's project to Oak Ridge "had not been preceded by a request for proposal, that there was no peer review of the contractors, no reseach protocol, and no principal investigator."[34]

Defenders of the government, including some of Mancuso's former colleagues, question the quality of his work and imply he has made an issue of himself in order to retain funding.[35] Similar charges and counter-charges surround Dr. Bross, whose study of pre-natal cancer induction was terminated after an unfavorable peer review organized by the National Cancer Institute.

The president's Inter-Agency Task Force on Radiation recommended in a final report issued June 20 that research into the health effects of radiation be centralized in the Department of Health, Education and Welfare (HEW), which presumably has no vested interest in the nuclear industry. HEW's National Institute for Occupational Safety and Health already is following up on Dr. Najarian's Portsmouth shipyard work with a more intensive study, and it contracted with Dr. Mancuso on Aug. 1 to continue his research for one more year. But Joseph A. Califano Jr. had not followed up on the task force's recommendations with a report to President Carter when he vacated his office as HEW secretary on Aug. 3. Radiation research, therefore, still is not centralized in an authority which is generally recognized as impartial.

---

[34] See Constance Holden's "Low-Level Radiation: A High-Level Concern," *Science*, April 13, 1979, p. 156.

[35] See Lapp, *op. cit.*, pp. 171ff for correspondence with Mancuso's collaborators.

The quest for reform of government research into radiation reflects a hope that it may still be possible to resolve the key issues by calm, scientific means, and yet this may well be a vain hope. Alvin M. Weinberg, who called nuclear energy a "Faustian bargain," has observed:

> The whole question of low-level radiation is so critical to public acceptance of nuclear energy that I consider this a leading, if not *the* [Weinberg's emphasis] leading, scientific issue underlying the nuclear controversy. Unfortunately, since the effects (if any) are so rarely seen because the exposures are so small, the issue may be beyond the ability of science to decipher.[36]

It will in any case be years before science is able to produce radiation research which all experts will recognize as definitive, and in the meantime policy decisions regarding not only nuclear energy but also nuclear war strategy and medical practices must be taken.

Decisions in Absence of Definitive Findings

Even if the risks associated with low-level radiation were precisely known, the policy decisions now facing the United States would involve painful choices. Some people invariably must bear a disproportionate amount of the risk that use of radiation entails, and somehow it must be determined how much risk certain social benefits are worth. There seems to be no way of making such determinations without ultimately putting a price on human life, and yet a cold calculation of this kind necessarily violates strong sentiments about the sanctity of life.

In terms of loss of life, the worst nuclear reactor accident in the United States occurred at the SL-1 experimental reactor in Idaho on Jan. 3, 1961, killing three workmen. This was not a large loss of life by the standards prevailing, say, in coal mining. Even so, the Idaho accident was in some ways uniquely troubling. The reactor building was so intensely radioactive following the accident that the bodies initially could not be removed. Twenty days elapsed before they could be safely handled for burial. Even then they had to be interred in lead coffins.

Is it worse to die in this fashion than in an accident on the Ohio Turnpike? David L. Bazelon, the noted circuit judge on the U.S. Court of Appeals for the District of Columbia, has observed that in primitive societies a shaman or wizard claiming special or miraculous insight would make such decisions. Scientists today, the judge believes, "must resist the temptation to belittle . . . concerns, however irrational they may seem." While scientists can contribute much to discussion of risks such as those arising from radiation, ultimately people have to decide for themselves how they feel and what they think. As for those

---

[36] Alvin M. Weinberg, "Nuclear Energy: Salvaging the Atomic Age," *The Wilson Quarterly*, summer 1979, p. 107.

who think the public is incapable of understanding the issues involved, Judge Bazelon invokes the words of Thomas Jefferson: "I know no safe depository of the ultimate powers of the society but the people themselves; and if we think them not enlightened enough to exercise their control with a wholesome discretion, the remedy is not to take it from them, but to inform their discretion."[37]

---

[37] David L. Bazelon, "Risk and Responsibility," *American Bar Association Journal*, July 1979, pp. 1066-1069.

Selected Bibliography

Books

Caldicott, Helen, *Nuclear Madness*, Autumn Press, 1978.
Lapp, Ralph E., *The Radiation Controversy*, Reddy Communications Inc., 1979.
Metzger, H. Peter, *The Atomic Establishment*, Simon & Shuster, 1972.
Union of Concerned Scientists, *The Nuclear Fuel Cycle*, MIT Press, 1975.

Articles

Bross, I. D. J., "Leukemia from Low-Level Radiation," *New England Journal of Medicine*, July 20, 1972.
Morgan, Karl Z., "Cancer and Low Level Ionizing Radiation," *The Bulletin of the Atomic Scientists*, September 1978.
Mancuso, T. F., Alice Stewart and George W. Kneale, "Radiation Exposure of Hanford Workers Dying from Cancer and Other Causes," *Health Physics*, Nov. 5, 1977.
Najarian, Thomas, and Theodore Colton, "Mortality from Leukemia and Cancer in Shipyard Nuclear Workers," *Lancet*, May 13, 1978.
Rotblat, Joseph, "The Risks for Radiation Workers," *The Bulletin of the Atomic Scientists*, September 1978.
Stewart, Alice, and George W. Kneale, "Radiation Dose Effects in Relation to Obstetric X-rays and Childhood Cancer," *Lancet*, June 5, 1970.

Reports and Studies

Effect of Radiation on Human Health, hearings before the Subcommittee on Health and the Environment of the Committee on Interstate and Foreign Commerce, House of Representatives, 95th Congress, January-February 1978, Serial Nos. 95-179 and 95-180, U.S. Government Printing Office, 1979.
Nuclear Power: Issues and Choices, report of the (Ford Foundation's) Nuclear Energy Policy Group, Ballinger, 1977.
Plutonium and the Workplace, prepared by Kitty Tucker and Eleanor Walters for the Environmental Policy Institute, Washington, D.C., March 1979.
Radiation Standards and Public Health, proceedings of a Second Congressional Seminar on Low-Level Ionizing Radiation, sponsored by The Congressional Environmental Study Conference, The Environmental Policy Institute and The Atomic Industrial Forum, Washington, D.C., Feb. 10, 1978.

ASSASSINATIONS INVESTIGATION

by

William V. Thomas

**Apr. 6
1979**

(**Report update:** The House Special Assassinations Committee concluded in its final report on July 17, 1979, that conspiracies played a role in the deaths of John F. Kennedy and Martin Luther King Jr. The committee, which spent two years and $5.4 million investigating the deaths, was unable to pinpoint any specific conspiracy; however, it did criticize agencies involved in earlier investigations for not pursuing information that allegedly could have uncovered such plots.)

ASSASSINATIONS INVESTIGATION

W HO KILLED John F. Kennedy?" is a question that will not go away. In the 15 years since the assassination, a wide variety of theories — some convincing, some bizarre — have been offered to explain how President Kennedy was murdered and why. Today, few Americans are without opinions on the subject. Amid a welter of conflicting speculation, a special Assassinations Committee was established nearly three years ago by the House of Representatives to re-examine the details of the case. But like so many past attempts to solve the mystery of what happened in Dallas, the committee may have raised more doubts than it put to rest.

At the conclusion of its hearings in December, the committee agreed with the basic findings of the Warren Commission *(see p. 90)* — that Lee Harvey Oswald fired three shots and the third shot killed the President — but it also announced the results of an acoustical study that seemed to show that four shots, not three, were fired at Kennedy. If the "noise analysis" is correct, a fourth shot would lend credence to the theory that there was another gunman besides Oswald, whom the Warren Commission named the sole assassin. Investigators have determined that Oswald's rifle could not have been fired and reloaded quickly enough for four shots to be fired from it in the 5.6 seconds that elapsed between the time the first and final shots were heard.

"Scientific acoustical evidence establishes a high probability that two gunmen fired at President John F. Kennedy," the committee said in a summary report issued Dec. 31. The report then concluded that the president was "probably assassinated as a result of a conspiracy." There matters have remained while the committee has prepared to issue a final report, which may or may not throw further light on the new questions it has raised. The final report, originally due March 30, is expected to be made public in late April or early May.

A host of conspiracy theories posed by critics of the Warren Commission's account of Kennedy's murder provided the central focus of the House committee's work. Its principal function, though, said Chief Counsel G. Robert Blakey, was to allay public suspicion of a cover-up by tying together "the loose ends" of the 26-volume Warren Report. One week after Kennedy was shot, 52 percent of the public, according to a Gallup Poll, believed that more than one person was responsible for the president's death. The belief in a lone assassin apparently has lost even more adherents since then. In February 1977, only 11 percent of those interviewed still thought that Oswald was the only gunman. The overwhelming majority, 81 percent, were convinced some other person or group of persons took part in the murder.[1]

In its investigation of the 1968 murder of Dr. Martin Luther King Jr. *(see p. 96)* the committee determined that there was a "likelihood" that the convicted assassin, James Earl Ray, participated in a conspiracy to kill the civil rights leader. The committee made no mention of any other gunman being involved in King's death, but based its conclusion on what it regarded as Ray's hope of receiving a sum of money for killing King. It stated flatly that the Central Intelligence Agency, the Federal Bureau of Investigation and the Secret Service were not involved in the Kennedy or King murders, although all were criticized for shortcomings in their original investigations. The committee recommended that the Justice Department review its findings and determine "whether further official examination is warranted in either case."

Dispute Over Accuracy of New Evidence

Almost as soon as the Assassinations Committee said that a fourth bullet might have been fired at President Kennedy, the accuracy of the new evidence was challenged — and defended. Evidence of the additional shot came from a recording made at the time of the assasssination when a motorcycle patrolman inadvertently turned his radio transmitter on. A recording of the sound transmitted on the radio was examined for the committee by acoustical experts Marck Weiss and Ernest Achkensay of Queens College in New York. Committee Chairman Louis Stokes, D-Ohio, said the committee was "very impressed" with their analysis.

Some members of the Dallas Police Department were decidedly not impressed. They contended that the motorcycle with the open microphone was not in Dealey Plaza where the President was shot, but two blocks away. The acoustical experts insisted that the transmitter had to be in Dealey Plaza.

The committee's assertion that a second gunman may have fired at Kennedy from the front has also been challenged. "There is only one place where people saw a gunman and that was the School Book Depository [behind the president's limousine]," said David W. Belin, former assistant counsel for the

[1] The Gallup Opinion Index, February 1977, p. 2.

Was Oswald Lying?

Movies and tape recordings have played an important part in helping investigators probe the complexities of the Kennedy assassination. In 1973, George O'Toole, a former CIA computer specialist and author of the book *The Assassination Tapes* (1975), subjected a recording of an interview with Lee Harvey Oswald to a voice analysis. The results, some have suggested, cast further doubt on the Warren Commission's conclusion that Oswald murdered President Kennedy.

O'Toole's instrument was the psychological stress evaluator (PSE), a lie-detector device. Unlike the widely used polygraph machine that monitors four body changes (pulse, blood pressure, breathing and sweating), the PSE detects subtle, inaudible voice changes produced when a person is under stress.

In contrast to the complex machinery used in a polygraph examination, a tape recorder is the only piece of equipment needed for a PSE test. The test may be conducted over the telephone or with any tape recording of a person's voice. Thus, O'Toole was able to "test" Lee Harvey Oswald. He obtained a tape recording in which the following exchange took place after Oswald's arrest:

Reporter: "Did you shoot the President?"
Oswald: "I didn't shoot anybody, no sir."

After processing the recording with the PSE, O'Toole found that Oswald's "categorical denial that he shot anyone contains almost no stress at all. . . . The psychological stress evaluator said he was telling the truth."

Warren Commission. "When the police went inside and searched the building . . . where people saw the gunman, they saw three cartridge cases and . . . a rifle. Those cartridge cases as well as the bullets found in the presidential limousine and the bullet [found on Kennedy's stretcher] at Parkland Hospital came from that rifle, which was Oswald's rifle, to the exclusion of all weapons in the world."[2]

Twenty-one witnesses told the Warren Commission that they thought at least one shot was fired from the grassy knoll in front of the presidential motorcade, but no weapon or gun shells were ever found in the area. "It seems to me," said Belin, "that you have to put the supposed second gunman into context of all of the evidence. Here is a gunman that no one ever sees, although people did see one firing from above. He fires a bullet, but no cartridge case is ever found. He misses not only the president, but he misses the entire limousine . . . from 100 or 125 feet away. . . . He fires only once. He then vanishes and disappears. You have lots of things which when you put them together really show that there is no support for a second gunman."

[2] David Belin, interviewed on "Meet the Press" (NBC-TV), Feb. 4, 1979.

The tape analysis the committee offered as evidence of a fourth gunshot may seem convincing at first, Belin said. But there are several problems. "The tape has sounds of chimes, which aren't in Dealey Plaza; the tape doesn't have the noises of the motorcycles revving up as they speed off to Parkland Hospital; the tape doesn't have the sounds of police sirens . . . , and the final thing is that theoretically everyone in that motorcade was on Channel 2 and the tape is on Channel 1."

Although some defenders of the Warren Commission's Report concede the possibility of a conspiracy, they point out that evidence supporting Oswald's guilt is overwhelming. Ballistics tests have shown that Oswald's rifle was the murder weapon, Oswald's fingerprints were on the rifle and on the part of the room where the rifle and spent cartridges were found; X-rays, photographs and the autopsy show that the bullets that killed Kennedy came from the area where Oswald was located; and after the shooting Oswald fled the building and resisted arrest by killing a policeman.

Conflicting Portrayals of the 'Real' Oswald

In the flood of books that followed the Kennedy assassination Lee Harvey Oswald was depicted as everything from a hapless loner and a dupe to a trained foreign agent. Since then Oswald's life and death have taken on the aspects of a puzzle complicated by years of guesswork and debate over his "real" identity. The picture of Oswald the Warren Commission accepted was of a withdrawn, mixed-up 24-year-old man who killed Kennedy for a combination of personal and political reasons. Oswald, a former Marine, defected to the Soviet Union in 1959 and returned to the United States in 1962. Killing Kennedy, the commission concluded, was the culmination of more than a year of troubles and frustrations for Oswald, during which he lost several jobs, became separated from his wife, and tried without success to kill Maj. Gen. Edwin Walker, at the time a spokesman for conservative political causes.

Oswald's wife, Marina Oswald Porter, confirmed this portrait of her husband. "His personality was constantly changing for the worst," she said. "I believe he was capable of doing such things [as killing the president]." But "I do not believe he would confide in someone. He was not that open a person." Oswald assassinated Kennedy, she added, because "he wanted to be somebody, wanted to be recognized."[3]

Many critics have rejected this account, choosing instead to see Oswald in a more sinister light. One of the most elaborate theories attempting to explain Oswald's behavior comes from a

---

[3] Testifying before the House Assassinations Committee, Sept. 13, 1979.

long-time critic of the Warren Commission, Edward J. Epstein. In his book *Legend: The Secret World of Lee Harvey Oswald* (1978), Epstein suggested that Oswald was recruited to spy for the Russians while he was serving as a Marine in Japan. Oswald had access to information on the U-2 reconnaissance plane that the Soviets wanted, the author theorized. After defecting to Russia, Oswald was trained in a Minsk spy school, Epstein contended, and later was sent back to the United States under the guise of being dissatisfied with Russian life. Epstein maintained that Oswald supplied the Russians with intelligence on anti-Castro activities in this country, an undertaking which may have led to his being "set up" by others who wished the president murdered.[4]

One fact militating against the idea that Soviet agents ordered Oswald to kill Kennedy is that he could be easily traced back to them. If Oswald did shoot the president, Epstein argued, he probably was acting on his own without the approval or knowledge of his superiors. The Assassinations Committee after examining all "available" evidence, however, could find no basis for believing that the Soviet government was involved in Kennedy's death or that Oswald ever worked for the Russians.

Suspicion of Mafia in Kennedy-Ruby Deaths

Critics of the Warren Report have long considered Oswald's murder by Dallas nightclub owner Jack Ruby to be the most important indication of the existence of a plot to kill President Kennedy. In September, the Assassinations Committee took up the question of Ruby's underworld ties, unearthing leads which, according to Chief Counsel Blakey, suggest that "some rogue elephant" subgroup within the Mafia may have engineered Kennedy's murder.[5]

Committee investigators found that Ruby had made a large number of "suspicious" telephone calls to alleged crime syndicate figures in the months preceding the assassination. Blakey said the investigators learned that Ruby had made calls in the summer and fall of 1963 to associates of Florida underworld leader Santos Trafficante and Mafia bosses Sam Giancana and Carlos Marcello. Many of the calls apparently dealt with labor troubles at Ruby's Dallas nightclubs, but 13 were made to people with established links to organized crime. Seven of the calls were to Lewis J. McWillie, whom Ruby visited in 1959 when he was working in an "organized-crime-controlled casino" — as described by the committee — in Havana. Ruby also

---

[4] Oswald's probable American contact, according to Epstein, was George de Morhrenschildt, a Russian emigre living in Dallas. De Morhrenschildt committed suicide in 1977 while an Assassination Committee investigator was waiting to interview him.

[5] Quoted in *The Atlantic*, March 1979.

called Irwin S. Weiner, a Chicago Mafia figure, and Nofio J. Pecora, allegedly a close associate of Texas syndicate chieftain Carlos Marcello.

In related testimony, Cuban exile José Aleman told the committee that Trafficante boasted to him that "Kennedy was going to be hit."[6] Aleman said he met Trafficante in the summer of 1963 to talk about business, but that Trafficante instead spent hours talking about the Kennedy administration's investigation of organized crime and Teamsters Union activities. At one point, Aleman testified, Trafficante told him there was no doubt Kennedy was not going to be re-elected. When Aleman disagreed, Trafficante replied: "You don't understand me. He's going to be hit." Trafficante, who appeared before the committee Sept. 28, denied having any prior knowledge of the Kennedy assassination or ever telling Aleman that Kennedy would be "hit."

Oswald's possible connection to organized crime is based on his relationship with three men in 1963: Charles Murret, David W. Ferrie and W. Guy Bannister. Murret and Ferrie were closely associated with Marcello's gambling operations in Louisiana and Texas. Bannister, an ex-FBI agent, was a go-between for the CIA and Cuban exiles involved in anti-Castro activities. Oswald, Ferrie and Bannister all occupied offices in the same New Orleans building in the spring and summer of 1963, and for a time during that period Oswald lived with Murret.

It would have been an easy matter, some contend, for Trafficante and Marcello, both angered by government action against them (Marcello was deported to Guatemala in 1961), to arrange for Kennedy's murder. Given their motive, it is entirely possible, experts say, that either or both of these men employed Oswald to kill the president, and later used Ruby to "silence" him after the assassination.[7]

Challenges to Past Findings

FEW OTHER occurrences in contemporary history have had as much personal impact on Americans as the assassination of President Kennedy. Even now, more than 15 years after Kennedy's death, most adults can remember exactly what they were doing when they first heard the shocking news. In part, the

---

[6] Testimony before the House Assassinations Committee, Sept. 27, 1978.
[7] See Carl Oglesby and Jeff Goldberg, "Did the Mob Kill Kennedy?" *The Washington Post*, Feb. 25, 1979. Oglesby and Goldberg are co-directors of the Assassination Information Bureau, an independent clearinghouse for assassination data.

Texas School Book Depository

Window from which Oswald is said to have shot Kennedy

HERTZ RENT A CAR CHEVROLETS

Dealey Plaza

Grassy Knoll

Route of Motorcade

unique character of the event derived from its unexpected suddenness. But an equally important factor was the extensive media coverage it was given. Radio, television and film recorded nearly every aspect of the tragedy. The American public, wrote Professor Wilbur Schramm, was made "to feel instantly" a part of the events from beginning to end.[8]

The assassination itself has become a grotesque tableau in the American imagination. Accompanied in an open car by his wife, Jacqueline, and Texas Gov. and Mrs. John Connally, Kennedy was fatally shot while riding through Dallas in a motorcade. The fateful day was Friday, Nov. 22, 1963. Connally and a bystander were wounded in the shooting but recovered. Within an hour of the assassination, patrolman J. D. Tippit of the Dallas Police Department was also shot and killed. Witnesses to the Tippit shooting testified that they saw the assailant run into a movie theater, where he was arrested. Meanwhile, the police found a rifle equipped with a telescopic sight on the sixth floor of the Texas School Book Depository, which overlooked the scene of the Kennedy assassination. When workers in the building were questioned, it was learned that one of the employees was missing. The missing man was Lee Harvey Oswald — the same person apprehended for killing Tippit. Oswald was formally charged with the murders of President Kennedy and Officer Tippit, but throughout his interrogation denied he had anything to do with either killing.

On Sunday, Nov. 24, two days after the assassination, preparations were made to transfer Oswald from the city to the county jail. With television cameras in the basement of the municipal police building recording the event, Oswald was being

[8] Wilbur Schramm, "Communication in Crisis," *The Kennedy Assassination and the American Public* (1965), p. 4; Bradley S. Greenberg and Edwin B. Parker, eds.

led from the cell block to a nearby armored car. Suddenly, a
man stepped from the crowd and fired one shot point-blank into
his stomach. Two hours later, Oswald died in surgery at
Parkland Memorial Hospital, the same hospital where Kennedy
had been pronounced dead.

Oswald's murderer was identified as Jack Ruby. Ruby maintained that he had acted in a temporary fit of rage over the
death of the president. Nevertheless, on March 14, 1964, a jury
found him guilty of first-degree homicide and sentenced him to
be executed. The death sentence was never carried out. Ruby
died of cancer on Jan. 4, 1967.

Conclusions of Warren Commission Report

In order to ascertain all the facts and circumstances relating
to the Kennedy assassination, President Johnson five days after
Oswald's death created a special seven-man investigating
commission headed by U.S. Chief Justice Earl Warren. Others
appeared to the commission
were four senior members of
Congress, Sens. Richard B.
Russell, D-Ga., and John
Sherman Cooper, R-Ky.,
Reps. Hale Boggs, D-La.,
and Gerald R. Ford, R-
Mich., and Allen W. Dulles,
former director of the Central
Intelligence Agency, and
John J. McCloy, a senior
Wall Street lawyer who had
served several presidents in
various posts. Johnson in-
structed the panel "to satisfy
itself that the truth is known
as far as it can be discovered,
and to report its findings and
conclusions" to the American
people and the world.

THE
OFFICIAL
WARREN
COMMISSION
REPORT
ON THE
ASSASSINATION
OF
PRESIDENT
JOHN F. KENNEDY

The commission held its first meeting on Dec. 5, 1963. During
its 10-month investigation, it heard more than 550 witnesses and
examined hundreds of reports and documents totalling tens of
thousands of pages submitted by the FBI, the Secret Service,
the Texas Attorney General's office, and other federal and state
investigative agencies, and the Dallas Police Department. The
commission's final report, submitted on Sept. 24, 1964, contained the following conclusions:

> 1. "The shots which killed President Kennedy and wounded
> Governor Connally were fired from the sixth-floor window at the
> southeast corner of the Texas School Book Depository."

Warren Commission members (from left): Dulles, Boggs, Cooper, Warren, Russell, McCloy and Ford.

2. "There is very persuasive evidence . . . to indicate that the same bullet which pierced the President's throat also caused Governor Connally's wounds."

3. "The shots which killed President Kennedy and wounded Governor Connally were fired by Lee Harvey Oswald."

4. "The Commission has found no evidence that either Lee Harvey Oswald or Jack Ruby was part of any conspiracy, domestic or foreign, to assassinate President Kennedy."

5. "All of the evidence before the Commission established that there was nothing to support the speculation that Oswald was an agent, employee, or informant of the FBI, CIA or any other governmental agency."

6. "On the basis of the evidence before the Commission, it concludes that Oswald acted alone."

In defense of the report a decade later, McCloy said in a CBS-TV interview, "I never saw a case more completely proven. There wasn't a scintilla of evidence that came along to the Warren Commission" that hinted at a conspiracy. McCloy added that he and other commission members "went down to Dallas thinking there must be a conspiracy. The president was shot and a couple of days later the [person] that shot him was killed. A strange sort of thing. But . . . we couldn't find any connection, and I don't think anybody could. The direct evidence was so overpowering that I didn't have any doubts about it when I got through."[9] Sen. Edward M. Kennedy, D-Mass., the slain president's brother, has said that he and his family "are satisfied with the Warren Report."[10] However, the commission's

---

[9] From an interview broadcast on CBS-TV, July 13, 1975. McCloy is one of the three surviving members of the Warren Commission. The others are Ford and Cooper.
[10] Quoted in *Skeptic* (now *Politics Today*), September-October 1975, p. 64. A spokesman for the senator said in March 1979 that he continues to stand by the statement.

findings, particularly its conclusion that Oswald acted alone, became the source of a continuing controversy.

Criticism of the Report's One-Assassin Finding

"Discrepancies, distortions and misrepresentations of crucial points of evidence are sufficient, even on a selective rather than a comprehensive basis, to condemn the Warren Report," wrote Sylvia Meagher, an early critic of the commission's findings. "The commission . . . issued a false indictment. It . . . accused Lee Harvey Oswald, after first denying [him a] posthumous defense and then systematically manipulating the evidence to build the case against him. . . . There is no indication in the vast collection of documentation that the commission at any time seriously considered the possibility that Oswald was not guilty, or that he had not acted alone."[11]

Of all the commission's conclusions, perhaps the one that has created the most controversy is the "single bullet" theory — that one of the three bullets believed fired at Kennedy struck him just below the neck, passed through him and then hit Gov. Connally, who was sitting directly in front of the president. The bullet, according to the commission, entered Connally's back, exited through his chest and struck his wrist and thigh. The two other bullets were accounted for, and tests performed on the murder weapon, an Italian-made Mannlicher-Carcano rifle, indicated that Oswald could not have reloaded it fast enough to hit Kennedy and Connally with separate shots.

Those who scoff at the "single bullet" explanation have pointed out that the bullet was recovered in almost perfect condition. Several experts have also taken issue with the commission's claim that the third shot hit Kennedy from behind. They maintain that he was struck in the head from the front by a bullet which — they theorize — was fired by a second gun, possibly from the direction of the grassy knoll near the motorcade route.

"I never believed that Oswald acted alone," President Johnson was quoted as saying in an interview published after his death in 1973, "although I can accept that he pulled the trigger."[12] Connally on several occasions disagreed with the commission's finding that he and Kennedy were hit by the same bullet. Testifying before the House Assassinations Committee on Sept. 6, however, he said it "might well be" that the single bullet theory was correct after all and that he and Kennedy were hit by the same shot. Three members of the commission were also reported to be doubtful of the "single bullet" conclusion

---

[11] Sylvia Meagher, "Notes for a New Investigation," *Esquire*, December 1966, p. 66.

[12] Quoted by Leo Janos, "The Last Days of the President," *The Atlantic*, July 1973.

Assassination 'Industry'

Since 1964, when the Warren Commission made public its conclusion that there was "no evidence of a conspiracy in the death of President Kennedy," about 300 books and 3,500 articles have been written about the assassination, most of them attacking the commission's methods or its findings.

One of the first such articles to appear was published in December 1963 in the *National Guardian* under the title "Oswald Innocent? — A Lawyer's Brief." The author was Mark Lane, who recently was back in the news as attorney to the late Jim Jones, leader of the Peoples Temple cult.

Shortly after the assassination, Lane made arrangements with Lee Harvey Oswald's mother to take on a posthumous defense of her son. Although the Warren Commission did not let him formally argue Oswald's case, Lane was quick to attack the panel's final report. In 1966 he published the book *Rush to Judgment,* in which he not only disputed the Warren Report's assertion of Oswald's guilt but argued that commission members overlooked many important facts in the case and deliberately covered up others.

In the intervening 13 years since the appearance of *Rush to Judgment,* many of Lane's arguments have been refuted. Nevertheless, his book, along with others challenging the official version of Kennedy's death, began a public debate on the assassination and its aftermath that shows no signs of subsiding.

and voiced their opposition. According to writer Milton Viorst, Sens. Cooper and Russell and Rep. Boggs all "reluctantly" signed the Warren Commission's report.[13]

New Orleans Trial of Clay Shaw in 1969

One of the most bizarre events to follow in the wake of the assassination was the trial of New Orleans businessman Clay Shaw on charges of conspiring to murder President Kennedy.

---

[13] Milton Viorst, "The Mafia, the CIA and the Kennedy Assassination," *Washingtonian,* November 1975, p. 87.

On March 1, 1967, New Orleans District Attorney Jim Garrison charged Shaw with masterminding a CIA plot to kill the president. He further alleged that the Warren Commission had deliberately covered up evidence establishing a conspiracy in the crime. When the trial began in February 1969, Garrison said that he would prove that Kennedy's murder was planned in New Orleans in the summer of 1963 by Shaw and others, including Oswald and David W. Ferrie. Ferrie was found dead of an apparent stroke in February 1967, several days after the investigation had been reported in the press.

Garrison's case against Shaw hung on the testimony of Perry Raymond Russo, who said he heard Oswald, Ferrie and a man introduced as "Clem Bertrand" (later identified as Shaw) discussing plans to assassinate Kennedy. The prosecution also offered as evidence of a conspiracy motion pictures of the assassination that had been filmed by Abraham Zapruder, a Dallas dress manufacturer who happened to be among the spectators along the motorcade route. It contended that the film, which seemed to show that Kennedy had been knocked backward against his seat when he was shot, was partial proof that he had been hit by a bullet fired from in front.

However, Oswald's widow testified for the defense that her husband had not known either Ferrie or Shaw. Other defense witnesses, an FBI firearms expert and an Army pathologist, upheld the Warren Commission conclusion that Kennedy was shot from behind. Dean A. Andrews Jr., a lawyer who initially told Garrison that he had been called by "Bertrand" and asked to defend Oswald for the murder of Kennedy, told the court he had made up the story. The jury acquitted Shaw of all charges. Subsequently, Shaw died and Garrison was defeated in his bid for re-election as district attorney. The outcome of the trial left critics of the Warren Report in temporary disarray.

Mood of Distrust Leading to New Inquiry

In the mid-1970s, revelations regarding the secret operations of the Central Intelligence Agency, the Federal Bureau of Investigation and the Nixon White House created a mood of mistrust among many Americans and helped to fan new interest in reopening hearings into the Kennedy assassination. Since the publication of the Warren Report, assassination buffs, writers and scholars had attacked the commission's conclusion that Lee Harvey Oswald acted alone in the slaying. But their demands for a new investigation were largely ignored by Congress until June 1976 when the Senate Select Intelligence Committee, as a byproduct of its investigation into CIA and FBI activities, issued a 106-page final report that suggested Kennedy's death might have been in retaliation for CIA attempts against the life of Cuban Premier Fidel Castro.[14]

Evidence pointing to this conclusion was never turned over to the Warren Commission by the CIA and the FBI, the report said. "The possibility exists that senior officials in both agencies made conscious decisions not to disclose potentially important information," according to the committee. But the committee said it had not been able to determine why the commission was not fully informed of the CIA's plotting against Castro.[15]

Public opinion polls released at the time the intelligence report came out indicated that nearly two-thirds of the American people doubted the Warren Commission's assertions. More than 80 members of the House of Representatives sponsored resolutions calling for a new investigation. "I can't say the commission was wrong in finding that Oswald acted alone and that there was no conspiracy," said Sen. Richard S. Schweiker, R-Pa., chairman of the Select Intelligence Committee. "But I'm convinced that the FBI and the CIA covered up evidence that was material to its investigation. We have not been told the whole truth."[16]

The House in September 1976 approved the creation of a special committee on assassinations to investigate the deaths of President Kennedy and civil rights leader Martin Luther King Jr. Almost from the outset, though, the investigation was marked by administrative bickering. Hearings were delayed for more than six months after a rift developed between committee Chairman Henry B. Gonzalez, D-Texas, and Chief Counsel Richard Sprague, a former assistant district attorney in Philadelphia.

Sprague's intended use of lie detectors and stress evaluators, plus his proposal for a first-year budget of $6.5 million — about six times larger than the House had expected — eroded support for the investigation. Gonzalez, blocked by the committee in his attempt to fire Sprague early in 1977, resigned. With House approval of the investigation in doubt, Sprague submitted his resignation. Hearings finally began that March under a new chairman, Rep. Louis Stokes, D-Ohio. G. Robert Blakey, a law professor and director of the Cornell Institute on Organized Crime, was appoint chief counsel.

---

[14] Castro has denied having any involvement in the assassination and in April 1978 told House Assassinations Committee investigators who had gone to Cuba that the idea would have been "insane." "That would have been the most perfect pretext for the United States to invade our country, which is what I have tried to prevent for all these years, in every way possible." Castro called "absurd" a report that he knew in advance of any assassination threat against Kennedy.

[15] See Senate Select Intelligence Committee, *Investigation of the Assassination of President John F. Kennedy: Performance of the Intelligence Agencies, Final Report*, June 23, 1976.

[16] Quoted by Mark R. Arnold in *The National Observer*, Nov. 1, 1975.

Added Causes of Public Doubt

THE TRAGIC events of 1963 seemed to repeat themselves with shocking familiarity in the spring of 1968 when Sen. Robert F. Kennedy, D-N.Y., brother of the slain president, and Dr. Martin Luther King Jr., the civil rights leader, were both assassinated. As murder followed murder, many people found it difficult to believe the killings were not in some way related. The attempted murder of Alabama Gov. George C. Wallace in 1972, as he campaigned for the Democratic presidential nomination, provided still more fuel for such suspicions.[17]

Sen. Kennedy, seeking the Democratic presidential nomination in 1968, was fatally shot on June 5 in a Los Angeles hotel at a celebration of his victory in the California primary election. The shooting occurred before dozens of people, and his assailant, Sirhan Birshara Sirhan, was immediately apprehended. He was tried for first-degree murder, found guilty and sentenced to death but his life was spared when the Supreme Court in 1972 (in *Furman v. Georgia*) struck down the death penalty in numerous states.

That Sirhan shot Kennedy was never in doubt. His trial, while it established his guilt, also functioned as a means of further informing the public about the crime. Nevertheless, speculation persisted that Kennedy's murder was a part of a conspiracy. Several witnesses said they saw a girl in a polka-dot dress run from the murder scene, the Ambassador Hotel in Los Angeles, shouting, "We've shot him. We've shot him." Others believed Sirhan was a member of the radical Palestinian organization Al Fatah, or that he was hired by mobsters to murder Kennedy. The Los Angeles police investigated 17 separate conspiracy theories, but could not substantiate any of them.[18]

Two days after Robert Kennedy's death, London police arrested James Earl Ray, who had been charged with shooting Dr. King. He was returned to Memphis, where the murder occurred, to be tried. But no trial was ever held. After first pleading innocent to the charges against him, Ray on March 10, 1969, entered a plea of guilty and was sentenced to 99 years in prison. Shortly afterward, though, Ray said he was coerced by his lawyer, Percy Foreman, to drop his not-guilty plea. Ray has spent the past decade trying without success to persuade the courts to re-hear his case.

---

[17] Wallace, shot at a political rally in Laurel, Md., May 15, 1972, was left paralyzed below the waist. Arthur Bremmer, an unemployed dish washer, was convicted of the shooting and sentenced to life in the Maryland State Penitentiary in Baltimore.

[18] See Robert A. Houghton, *Special Unit Senator: The Investigation of the Assassination of Senator Robert F. Kennedy* (1970).

To be sure, there are several unanswered questions about Ray's role in the King assassination. If Ray was acting on his own, as many believe, why did he leave the murder weapon and other evidence easily traceable to him at the scene of the crime? Where did Ray, who had been unemployed since escaping from the Missouri State Prison in April 1967, get the money to pay for his extensive travels before and after the assassination? Ray admitted that he bought the rifle that killed King and drove the getaway car. However, the actual murder, he claimed, was committed by a man from Montreal, Canada, whom he knew only as "Raoul."[19]

Re-Examining James Earl Ray's Role

Ray's appearance before the House Assassinations Committee, many believed, afforded him the opportunity he had always wanted to prove his innocence in the King murder. But he provided little or no new information to establish his innocence or implicate others in a conspiracy. Most of Ray's testimony focused on his relationship with Raoul, a mysterious figure who law-enforcement officials have never been able to identify and about whom they knew nothing other than what Ray has told them. Ray said he and Raoul had engaged in gun smuggling in the United States, Canada and Mexico after meeting in a Montreal bar in 1967. "I didn't make no effort to know him well," Ray said of Raoul. "That's a good way to get yourself killed." When pressed to prove the identity of Raoul, Ray had only vague answers about possible witnesses to his existence.

In light of Senate Intelligence Committee revelations in 1975 of attempts by J. Edgar Hoover to harass and defame Dr. King, the committee examined various theories of direct or indirect FBI involvement in King's murder. But Chief Counsel Blakey concluded that there "was no evidence" of any contact between Ray and the agency before King was killed. Disputing the contention that the original investigation was flawed, a retired Memphis FBI agent, William Lawrence, testified that the probe was "conducted as thoroughly and fairly as any could be." It was "one of the seven or eight most intensive investigations ever pursued by the bureau."[20] Robert Jensen, who headed the FBI's Memphis office at the time of the King assassination, said several conspiracy theories were investigated, including involvement by the Mafia, the Ku Klux Klan or a communist government. But none was proven.

In its preliminary report issued in December 1978, the com-

---

[19] See Bynum Shaw, "Are You Sure Who Killed Martin Luther King?" *Esquire,* March 1972, p. 114; see also William Bradford Huie's, *He Slew the Dreamer* (1968).

[20] Testimony of William Lawrence before House Assassinations Committee, Nov. 21, 1978.

mittee said it was "highly probably that . . . Ray stalked Dr. King for a period immediately preceding the assassination." The committee also said that on the basis of available evidence "there is a likelihood that . . . Ray assassinated Dr. King as a result of a conspiracy."

Alluding to a much-publicized $50,000 price that supposedly had been put on King's head by two St. Louis businessmen, both now dead, the committee concluded that word of the bounty may have reached the Missouri State Prison where Ray was an inmate. Ray could have acted with the intention of being paid, Blakey said, but "there is no evidence that he ever received payment." Percy Foreman, Ray's attorney, testified that Ray told him there was no conspiracy to kill King. Ray acted on his own, Foreman said. "[He thought] shooting Dr. King would make him a hero . . . the white hope."[21]

Conspiracy Theories; Their Basic Causes

"Human kind cannot bear very much reality," poet T.S. Eliot observed.[22] In one respect at least, that intolerance may explain the persistent beliefs in assassination conspiracies. Author William J. Crotty has suggested that many individuals are eager to believe in conspiracies because the alternative is too frightening: "[It is] difficult to understand how one demented gunman can bring down a powerful leader. . . . A pressing necessity exists to explain [such a] murder in broader and more acceptable terms, rather than as a quirk happening."[23] In the absence of a clear explanation of why certain traumatic events occur, people invent reasons of their own. In the case of the Kennedy-King killings, the idea of an all-encompassing conspiracy gives motive and reason to otherwise shocking catastrophes.

The tendency to espouse conspiracy theories has been encouraged not only by the nature of the assassinations themselves but also by the official versions of how and why they happened. "One of the troubling things about the Kennedy case," said Robert Blakey, "is that we never had a trial. We never had our Greek tragedy."[24] Classical tragedy gathers up loose ends of complicated situations and ties them neatly together. The Warren Commission, many now believe, did not do that. They stated their opinion "as if they mistrusted the American public," Blakey said. "They should have said, 'We've done the best we could, we know who shot the president, we're not sure whether others were involved,' and then trusted . . . the maturity of the American people to accept [that judgment]. They

---

[21] Testimony before the House Assassinations Committee, Nov. 13, 1978.
[22] From "Burnt Norton," *Four Quartets* (1943).
[23] William J. Crotty, *Assassination and the Political Order* (1971), p. 265.
[24] Quoted in *The Atlantic*, March 1979.

didn't. And this let into our society a kind of poison that has run through the body politic ever since."

If there is a message to be drawn from this experience, Blakey added, "it can be summed up in two words — *never again!* The next time this happens . . . I hope indeed that people will have the courage and integrity to stand up and say, 'I will pursue this as far as I can. . . .'"[25] Sadly, since nine[26] of the 38 American presidents have been shot or shot at, the test of how far we are willing to pursue the truth may come sooner than anyone would wish.

---

[25] Speaking in New York, Jan. 25, 1979.
[26] Andrew Jackson, Abraham Lincoln, James Garfield, William McKinley, Theodore Roosevelt, Franklin D. Roosevelt, Harry S Truman, John F. Kennedy, Gerald R. Ford. Of these, four were assassinated: Lincoln, Garfield, McKinley and Kennedy. Carter is considered the 39th president but only 38 men have held the office. Grover Cleveland served twice, 1885-89 and 1893-97, becoming the 22nd and 24th president.

Selected Bibliography
Books

Belin, David W., *November 22, 1963: You Are the Jury*, Quadrangle, 1973.

Crotty, William J., ed., *Assassinations and the Political Order*, Harper & Row, 1971.

Epstein, Edward J., *Inquest: The Warren Commission and the Establishment of Truth*, Viking, 1966.

—— *Legend: The Secret World of Lee Harvey Oswald*, Reader's Digest/McGraw Hill, 1978.

Ford, Gerald R., *Portrait of the Assassin*, Simon and Shuster, 1965.

Huie, William B., *Did the FBI Kill Martin Luther King?* Nelson Press, 1977.

Lane, Mark, *Rush to Judgment*, Holt Rinehart & Winston, 1966.

—— *Code Name Zorro: The Murder of Martin Luther King, Jr.*, Prentice-Hall, 1977.

McKinley, James, *Assassination in America*, Harper & Row, 1977.

Meagher, Sylvia, *Accessories After the Fact*, Bobbs-Merrill, 1967.

Popkin, Richard, *The Second Oswald*, Avon, 1966.

Scott, Peter Dale, *The Assassinations: Dallas and Beyond — A Guide to Cover-ups and Investigations*, Vintage, 1976.

Wills, Garry and Ovid Demaris, *Jack Ruby*, New American Library, 1967.

Articles

Anson, Robert Sam, "The Greatest Cover-up of All," *New Times*, April 18, 1975.

Cohen, Jacob, "Conspiracy Fever," *Commentary*, October 1975.

Douglas, George H., "The Young Assassins," *The Nation*, June 19, 1972.

Epstein, Edward J., "The War of the Moles," *New York*, Feb. 27, 1978.

—— "Oswald: The Secret Agent," *New York*, March 6, 1978.

Lapham, Lewis H., "The Assassin as Celebrity," *Harper's*, November 1975.

Marx, Garry T., "Of Double Agents and Revolving Doors," *The New Republic*, Oct. 18, 1975.

Ridenour, Ron, "The Assassination of Martin Luther King, Jr.," *Skeptic*, March-April 1977.

Skeptic, entire issue, "Who Killed JFK?" September-October 1975.

Szulc, Ted, "The Warren Commission in Its Own Words," *The New Republic*, Sept. 27, 1975.

Webster, William H., "The Lincoln Assassination and its Investigation," *Vital Speeches*, March 15, 1979.

Reports and Studies

Commission on CIA Activities Within the United States, Report to the President, U.S. Government Printing Office, June 1975.

Editorial Research Reports: "Presidential Protection," 1975 Vol. II. p. 905.

Meagher, Sylvia, "Subject Index to the Warren Report and Hearings and Exhibits," Scarecrow Press, 1966.

The President's Commission on the Assassination of President John F. Kennedy, "Report," U.S. Government Printing Office, 1964.

U.S. House of Representatives Select Committee on Assassinations, Summary of Findings and Recommendations, Jan. 2, 1979.

CENSUS TAKING, 1980

by

John Kotler

**Feb. 29
1 9 8 0**

CENSUS TAKING, 1980

F OR THE 20th time since the nation's beginning, it will count its people in a decennial census and try to find out where and how they live. About 90 percent of the 80 million households will receive census questionnaires by mail with instructions to return them as close as possible to Census Day, April 1. The remaining people, mostly those in sparsely populated rural areas, will be visited in person by census enumerators. The goal of this massive effort is to provide a statistical portrait from which government and business will make decisions affecting them all. Where people live will determine which states will gain or lose congressional seats. It will also bear on the multi-billion-dollar allocation of federal and state funds to localities, on business plans for plant location and market strategy, on social needs for the aged, the inner city, the rural poor, and on a thousand other matters.

While complete, accurate and reliable statistical knowledge is essential for all of those purposes, the Census Bureau by its own admission has been unable in past censuses to find and count every man, woman and child. Census officials do not expect a perfect score this year either, but they hope to improve on their 1970 record. They estimate that 5.3 million people, 2.5 percent of the population, did not get counted that year. Even that was an improvement over 1950 and 1960.[1]

The bureau is mounting a special effort to count members of minority groups, which accounted for a disproportionately large segment of those missed 10 years ago. Census officials have estimated that 7.7 percent of all blacks were missed in 1970, compared to only 1.9 percent of the whites. The rate of undercount for black men is believed to have been nearly 10 percent. Although estimates of other ethnic and racial groups are less accurate, it is agreed that Hispanics and Asian-Americans were also undercounted.

The new effort to reach minorities encompasses several approaches. The Census Bureau has established special advisory committees to help it reach the racial and ethnic groups that figured prominently in the 1970 undercount. It also has sought to

---

[1] A panel sponsored by the National Academy of Sciences *(see p. 108)* reported that the census missed 5.1 million people (3.3 percent) in 1950 and that the 1960 census missed about the same number, but they represented a smaller percentage (2.7) of total population.

hire community relations specialists in minority communities. Moreover, many of the 275,000 temporary enumerators and office employees for the census are being drawn from minority groups.

The Census Bureau is relying on a free advertising program created by Ogilvy & Mather, the Madison Avenue advertising agency, and distributed by the Advertising Council, the national association of advertising agencies. Many of the advertisements include endorsements of the census by sports figures such as Luis Tiant of the New York Yankees and Elvin Hayes of the Washington Bullets. The ads stress the importance of being counted, and emphasize that census data on individuals is confidential by law. A Hispanic news organization, the Spanish International Network, plans to provide special programs endorsing and explaining the census to 36 affiliate stations.

In 1970 some of the more radical minority groups urged blacks and Hispanics not to be counted, saying the government would use the information to snoop on them.[2] But this time, the emphasis is clearly in the other direction. The Mexican-American Legal Defense and Education Fund has established nine offices to promote the 1980 census in Hispanic communities. Seven of the offices are in Texas, one of the southwestern states where Hispanics are likely to pick up new state legislative seats. Their other offices are in Illinois and California. Al Perez, the organization's Washington counsel, predicts the count in the Los Angeles area will assure the creation of a second congressional district in California populated predominantly by Mexican-Americans.[3]

Battle Over Count, Identity of Illegal Aliens

The effort to improve the count of minorities has led to a legal struggle over whether to include illegal aliens in the 1980 head count. The Federation for American Immigration Reform (FAIR), an organization with ties to Zero Population Growth and other population and environmental organizations, has filed a lawsuit in federal district court to prevent the Census Bureau from counting illegal aliens, or else, to require that it place them in a separate category for purposes of reapportionment. FAIR contends that counting them tends to "legitimize" illegal immigration and deprive states without substantial numbers of "undocumented" aliens of their rights to congressional representation and federal revenue.

FAIR has been joined in the suit by 20 members of Congress

---

[2] See "Census Taking, 1970," *E.R.R.*, 1970 Vol. I, pp. 203-218.
[3] Interview Feb. 6, 1980. In 1974, the predominantly Mexican-American communities of eastern Los Angeles were combined with downtown Los Angeles and the suburb East Los Angeles to form the 25th congressional district. The district is represented by Rep. Edward R. Roybal (D), a member of the Congressional Hispanic Caucus.

Illegal Aliens — How Many?

No one knows for certain how many illegal aliens there are in the United States. In recent years estimates have ranged from 3 million to 12 million. The Census Bureau estimated on Jan. 31 that the number was no greater than 5 million and might be as low as 3.5 million. The bureau also contends that the number from Mexico is lower than popularly believed — almost certainly less than 3 million and possibly between 1.5 and 2.5 million.* Jeffrey S. Passell, a Census Bureau demographer, said** illegal immigrants from Mexico are less likely than others to take up permanent residence in the United States. Most Mexican nationals who enter the country illegally return to Mexico for at least part of the year, he said.

The whereabouts of illegal aliens are even more uncertain than the total numbers, Passell said. During December 1978 and January 1979, the Mexican government surveyed Mexican households and asked if they had family members working or seeking work in the United States. The survey did not distinguish between those who had come to the United States legally and those here illegally. But Passell said it is likely that illegal immigrants are located in much the same places as legal aliens. The Mexican study produced roughly the same findings as a study by the Immigration and Naturalization Service in 1976-77. Here's where the studies indicated Mexican aliens — legal and illegal — were living:

Mexican Study		INS Study	
California	50.9%	California	48.8%
Texas	21.1	Texas	26.2
Illinois	7.9	Illinois	10.1
New Mexico	2.0	New Mexico	1.8
Colorado	1.8	Colorado	1.2
Arizona	1.7	Arizona	3.6
Oregon	1.2	Oregon	0.4
Florida	1.1	Florida	0.7
Other states	4.1	Other states	7.1
Not specified	8.1		

* Census estimates in a working paper prepared for the President's Select Committee on Immigration and Refugee Policy.
** Interview, Feb. 15, 1980.

from Pennsylvania, three from Illinois and one each from California, Vermont and Kentucky.[4] Many of the protestors fear that a full enumeration of illegal immigrants will result in losses of congressional districts in their states. The Committee for

[4] Pennsylvania — Sen. H. John Heinz (R); Reps. Eugene V. Atkinson (D), Don Bailey (D), William F. Clinger Jr. (R), Lawrence Coughlin (R), Charles F. Dougherty (R), Joseph M. Gaydos (D), Bill Goodling (R), Raymond F. Lederer (D), Marc L. Marks (R), Joseph M. McDade (R), Austin J. Murphy (D), John P. Murtha (D), Michael Myers (D), Donald Ritter (R), Richard T. Schulze (R), Bud Shuster (R), Doug Walgren (D), Robert S. Walker (R), and Gus Yatron (D); Illinois — Reps. Edward J. Derwinski (R), Paul Findley (R), and Henry J. Hyde (R); California — Rep. Clair W. Burgener (R); Kentucky — Sen. Walter Huddleston (D); Vermont — Rep. James M. Jeffords (R).

Representative Government, a black organization in California, has also joined the suit. The state of Vermont has filed a friend-of-the-court brief on behalf of the suit. The city and state of New York have petitioned to join the suit on behalf of the Census Bureau. Both believe they will lose congressional seats and federal revenue if illegal aliens are not included in the census count.[5]

Barnaby Zall of FAIR's Washington headquarters contends that to count illegal aliens would create a vested interest in lax immigration laws and law enforcement. "We would have congressmen who depend on illegal immigrants for their seats," he said. "They would work to loosen immigration laws, and we would end up institutionalizing illegal immigration."[6] Congress now forbids undocumented workers from participating in job training programs funded under the federal Comprehensive Employment and Training Act (CETA), but it does not specifically exclude them from some other federally funded programs.

The Census Bureau, on the other hand, argues that the Constitution (Article I, Section 2), clearly requires it to enumerate the "whole number" of persons in each state, without regard to their citizenship.[7] From a practical standpoint, bureau officials say it would be impossible to identify illegal aliens. Presumably none would admit to their status, despite the legal penalty for refusal to provide census information.[8] Census officials also contend that changes in the questionnaires at this time could delay the count and make it impossible to present new state population figures to the president on Jan. 1, 1981, as required by law.

In their efforts to coax illegal aliens into cooperating, the Census Bureau community liaison people stress that all information about individuals is strictly confidential.[9] While the census questionnaire does not ask if a person is in the country illegally, it does ask if he or she is a citizen and asks non-citizens when they entered the country. The questionnaire also seeks information about racial and ethnic identity.

---

[5] A hearing on the suit took place Feb. 7 before a special three-judge panel composed of two judges from the U.S. District Court in Washington, D.C. and one judge from the U.S. Circuit Court of Appeals. Law provides for the special panel in cases concerned with apportionment of federal and state voting districts. The panel's decisions, if appealed, go straight to the Supreme Court.

[6] Interview, Feb. 5, 1980.

[7] The Founding Fathers did exclude Indians who were not taxed. Slaves were assigned three-fifths the numerical value of free persons. Both of these exceptions were later abolished *(see p. 111)*. Today only diplomats and tourists from foreign countries are not counted.

[8] Current law provides for fines of $100 to $500 for individuals who refuse to answer the surveys or provide false answers. Until 1976, they could also be jailed for up to 60 days. That year Congress removed the criminal penalties but retained the civil fines. No one has ever been jailed for refusal to answer census questions though some have been fined.

[9] Federal law prohibits releasing census information about individuals. Violations can result in a fine and a jail sentence. A person may, under certain circumstances, gain access to his own census files. It is generally acknowledged that the Census Bureau has kept its vow of confidentiality. The bureau, for instance, refused to disclose information about Japanese-Americans during World War II. However, there was a lapse in World War I when the bureau provided information about men who claimed they were too old to be drafted.

The Census Bureau requested that U.S. leaders of the Catholic Church endorse the census and, in communities presumed to have many illegal aliens, ask the priests to counsel parishioners that they have nothing to fear from filling out census forms. The United States Catholic Conference declined to endorse the census formally, although it approved the objective of an accurate count. It is believed that Catholic leaders feared the church would lose credibility if they endorsed the census and the promise of confidentiality was broken.

Testing 1980 Questions and Mailing Lists

Stung by criticism of its undercount in 1970, the Census Bureau set out to remedy the situation well before 1980. It began planning the next census in 1974. Preparation included the testing of various census questionnaires and enumerating techniques in selected places around the country. On the basis of these and other findings, the bureau rewrote some questions and added new ones. Finally, it was decided that most households will receive a short version of the questionnaire, which consists of nine questions about the identity, marital status and ethnic background of each person in the household and 12 questions on housing. In deference to changing mores, there is no longer a designation for "head of household." Instead the husband or wife is simply listed as owner of the home. There is also a new category for "partner/roommate."

About one household in five has been selected at random to receive a long form which includes questions about energy use, transportation, employment, income and language use. The Census Bureau has issued a 61-page pamphlet detailing how each question relates to federal and local laws and programs.[10]

In its attempt to miss no one, the Census Bureau compiled an address register by purchasing commercial mailing lists and checking them against its own files and those of the U.S. Postal Service and other agencies. Enumerators will check many neighborhoods in person to make sure that the address list is complete. There will also be a follow-up to determine that all questionnaires are returned. Even further, the bureau designated two days for enumerating people who live in hotels, rooming houses, missions, and "street people" with no fixed addresses.[11]

As 1980 approached, it became clear that the Census Bureau would not escape controversy again. It has been criticized for

---

[10] "Summary Description of Data Use for Questions Planned for Inclusion in the 1980 Census," U.S. Department of Commerce, Bureau of the Census, February 1979.

[11] March 31 will be T(transient)-Night, when enumerators will go to hotels and motels charging more than $4 a night, YMCAs, YWCAs, campgrounds and the like. On April 8, M(mission)-Night, enumerators will count people in missions, flophouses and other places that charge less than $4 a night, and in local jails and detention centers where people are held for less than 30 days, and bus and railroad stations.

spending too much — and for not doing enough. Manuel D. Plotkin resigned as census director in February 1979, after two years on the job. *The New York Times* attributed his departure to pressure from the Carter administration amid "mounting concern over the bureau's ability to carry out the crucial 1980 count properly."[12] Plotkin was replaced by Vincent P. Barabba, who had directed the 1970 census. A year after Plotkin's departure, Earle J. Gerson was relieved of his duties overseeing the 1980 census count and was reassigned to another position. It was alleged in the press that Gerson had failed to inform his superiors that a private contractor hired to address census questionnaires had misapplied 20 percent of the labels.

Altogether, it is estimated that the 1980 census will cost in excess of $1 billion, more than four times the $221 million price tag in 1970. Even when adjusted for inflation, the 1980 cost is expected to double the 1970 figure. The cost of counting each person is expected to rise from $1.72 to more than $4, according to a report issued in 1978 by the General Accounting Office, the auditing arm of Congress.[13] The GAO concluded that the extra expenditures were planned "without assurance that there will be an appreciable improvement in the data collected." The report mentions an earlier GAO study which indicated that it was "doubtful" whether a substantial improvement could be made in the undercount.[14]

The Census Bureau has said that about half of the added cost of the 1980 census, after inflation is taken into account, is to improve the undercount. The GAO questioned whether the improvements would be great enough to justify the larger cost. However, a panel functioning under the auspices of the National Academy of Sciences concluded in its 1978 study of plans for the 1980 census that the extra costs were justified.[15] The study indicated that the census would be "generally effective" but it doubted the bureau's ability to achieve a full count in minority communities, especially where people are not fluent in English. While the bureau had made technical and procedural improvements in taking the census, the study added, it had not fully comprehended the importance of improving community relations and making adjustments for the life-style of minority communities. Census officials say there is only so much they can do to encourage people to cooperate.

[12] *The New York Times*, Feb. 12, 1980.
[13] "Bureau of the Census Planning, Budgeting, and Accounting for the 1980 Census," Dec. 11, 1978.
[14] "Programs to Reduce the Decennial Census Undercount," Report to the House Committee on Post Office and Civil Service by the comptroller general, May 5, 1976.
[15] "Counting the People in 1980: An Appraisal of Census Plans," The National Academy of Sciences, 1978. The 14-member panel consisted of minority group representatives and specialists in statistics, demography, city planning, surveys, communications and other fields related to census taking. The panel was headed by Nathan Keyfitz, chairman of the department of sociology and demography at Harvard University.

1980 Census of the United States

Here are the QUESTIONS ↓	These are the columns for ANSWERS ➤ Please fill one column for each person listed in Question 1.	PERSON in column 1		PERSON in column 2	
		Last name		Last name	
		First name	Middle initial	First name	Middle initial
2. How is this person related to the person in column 1? Fill one circle. If "Other relative" of person in column 1,		START in this column with the household member (or one of the members) in whose name the home is owned or rented. If there ~~no~~ such person, start in this column with		If relative of person in column 1 ○ Husband/wife ○ Father/mother ○ Son/daughter ○ Other relative ➤ ○ Brother/sister If no~~t re~~lated to person in column 1	

1980 Census Questions

Population
(every person)

Name, sex, age, marital status, racial/ethnic background, Spanish/Hispanic descent, relationship to home owner (the term "head of household" is not used in this questionnaire); school attendance, last grade completed. Also questions to determine if any person has been left out.

Housing
(every household)

Number of dwelling units in building; how one enters living quarters; plumbing facilities; number of rooms; own, rent or guest; whether building is condominium; size of lot; market value of home if single-family home or condominium; monthly rent.

(asked of every fifth person or household)

All those listed above, plus place of birth (state or foreign country); whether person naturalized citizen and when arrived in the United States; languages spoken besides English; ancestry; where person lived five years ago; (if born before April 1965) occupation five years ago, military service, physical or mental problems lasting more than six years, number of marriages; (for women) number of children; whether person worked during previous week (before April 1) and number of hours; address of work place; time it took to get to work from home and means of transportation; whether person is on layoff; when last worked; occupation; sources of income and total income for 1979; other questions.

Type of building (i.e. single-family home, mobile home, duplex, etc.); number of stories; elevator; size and type of lot; water source; connected to public sewerage facilities; type of heat; fuel used to heat home, water, for cooking; monthly utility bills; number of bedrooms, bathrooms (whether there is flush toilet, tub or shower and wash basin with running water); telephone; air conditioning; when building was constructed; when owner moved in; if single-family dwelling (condominiums, homes on more than 10 acres and some other categories not included) real estate taxes for 1979, fire and hazard insurance premiums, types of mortgage or debt on property, total monthly payment on property debt; other questions.

One controversial matter still to be decided is whether to make a statistical "adjustment" for the undercount. In past censuses, the count was final even if later studies indicated an undercount. The study for the National Academy of Sciences said that "adjustments in the population total would lead to greater equity in distribution of funds among the states" although it also acknowledged that an adjustment might produce figures for some areas "that are farther from the true population instead of closer." Although, on balance, the panel favored an adjustment, it did not propose a particular method.

Bryant Robey, editor of *American Demographics* magazine, opposes an official adjustment, saying that any changes are likely to be viewed as political maneuvering and that the new figures may be no closer to reality than the original count. Robey proposes instead that government officials pay more attention to later population estimates rather than relying on census figures alone in developing programs and disbursing funds.[16]

Development of the U.S. Census

THE EARLIEST enumerations were conducted to apportion taxes or assess military manpower. A population census for tax purposes took place in parts of China as early as 3000 B.C.; the children of Israel, upon their exodus from Egypt about 1300 B.C., ascertained their fighting strength by a count of males 20 years old or older, conducted by enumerators appointed by each tribe. There is also a biblical account of another census, conducted at the beginning of the first millennium B.C. by King David.

A few centuries later, Solon of Athens applied the Egyptian system, already ancient at that time, of listing people by occupation. Beginning in the sixth century B.C., the city of Rome counted its people and their property every fifth year. The Emperor Augustus extended the census to the entire Roman empire, for taxation, a fact well-remembered today because of its link in the New Testament account of the birth of Jesus. According to the Gospel of St. Luke, Joseph and Mary went from Galilee to Bethlehem for the census and while there she gave birth to the one whom Christianity worships as the Messiah, or Christ.

In the ninth century A.D., officers of Charlemagne produced a "breviary" or summary of the population and property in his

---

[16] Bryant Robey, "Adjusting for Census Undercount: The Statistical Nightmare," *American Demographics*, February 1980, pp. 18-23, 46.

kingdom. Royal investigators under William the Conqueror in 1086 carried out a listing of manors, proprietors, and peasants in England and recorded the results in the Domesday Book — so-called because no appeal against its findings was permitted. The first censuses in the New World were those conducted by the Spanish conquistadores in Peru in 1548 and Mexico in 1576. In British North America, colonial governors of Virginia had their people counted in 1624-25, 1634-35, and later years. Thirty censuses were recorded among the other 12 colonies and states between 1776 and 1790.

The United States, however, became the first modern nation to require a periodic numbering of its people. The Constitution, ratified in 1789, required a census every 10 years. From the beginning, the census had political importance beyond its value as a head count. It was the centerpiece of a "masterly compromise" which resulted in establishment of two houses of Congress.[17] After much debate, the Founding Fathers agreed to create one chamber, the Senate, where each state would have equal representation, and a second chamber, the House of Representatives, where each state would be represented according to its population.

Thus the decennial census became the vehicle for apportioning the seats of the House of Representatives "among the several States ... according to their respective Numbers" (Article I, Section 2). Congress in March 1790 enacted legislation requiring the first census, which was begun on the first Monday in August (Aug. 2) of the same year. Federal marshals who took that census, and several others, were obstructed by poor roads, hostile Indians, and a reluctance to answer the questions.

George Washington commented on the probable undercount in the first census in a letter to Gouverneur Morris in 1791. He ascribed it to "religious scruples of some ... fears of others that it [the census] was intended as the foundation of a tax ... indolence of the people, and the negligence of many of the [census] officers."[18] In contrast to the required secrecy of individual answers today, enumerators in the first census were required by law to post the returns in two of the most public places in the community. The first census reported 3,929,213 people, although at that time untaxed Indians were not counted and every five slaves were counted as only three persons.[19]

---

[17] See Gerald Carson's "The Great Enumeration" in *American Heritage*, December 1979, p. 8.

[18] *The Writings of George Washington* (edited by John C. Fitzpatrick, 1939), Vol. XXXI, p. 329.

[19] The census would be determined, according to the constitutional provision then in effect, "by adding the whole Number of free Persons, including those bound to Service for a Term of Years [indentured servants], and excluding Indians not taxed, three fifths of all other Persons." The term "other persons" meant slaves. This reference was made obsolete by the Thirteenth and Fourteenth Amendments adopted after the Civil War.

For the first six censuses, information about each family was summarized on one line and the only name listed was for the man who headed the household. But in 1850, for the first time, each person was listed on a separate line. Thus the individual rather than the family became the basic unit for the census. This single change was characterized by Dr. Walter F. Wilcox, who headed a study of the census in 1898 by the American Economic Association, as "perhaps the most important in the whole history of the census." In her history of the census, Ann Herbert Scott added in 1968: "[I]t furnished checks on the accuracy of enumeration and permitted the detailed tabulations which are the heart of census analysis."[20]

Growth of Goals During the 19th Century

James Madison had proposed asking people about their occupations in the first census, but his idea was passed over temporarily. Before the census of 1800, Thomas Jefferson and Timothy Dwight, president of the Connecticut Academy of Arts and Sciences, petitioned Congress for a "more detailed view of the inhabitants" in the belief that future generations would find it "highly gratifying to observe the progress of the population." Congress made provisions for listing free white men and women in five age categories in that census, but declined to seek any greater detail.

Ten years later, when America seemed to be on the verge of war with England, Congress authorized the first census of manufactures, included in the decennial census of 1810, to assess the country's economic strength. In 1820, the fourth decennial census, Congress finally took Madison's suggestion and authorized a question about occupations along with questions about agriculture and commerce.

Earlier censuses had made no distinction between citizens and foreigners. It was not until 1820 that the item "foreigner not naturalized" was included in the questions. This reflected the rise of a national consciousness and the stirrings of concern about immigration. "In later years, as newcomers multiplied, statistics on immigration became a matter of enormous public interest, and questions were added to cover birthplace and language or dialect spoken," Ann Herbert Scott wrote. Resident aliens never have been excluded from census counts.

In 1840, President Martin Van Buren, a former superintendent of the census, received congressional approval to add more questions. The questionnaire became so overloaded that the newly established (1839) American Statistical Association questioned the accuracy of the results. But the profusion of questions

---

[20] Ann Herbert Scott, *Census U.S.A.* (1968), p. 29.

continued. Censuses of mines and quarries were first conducted in 1840 along with the population census. In 1889 and 1890, some people had to answer as many as 470 questions, the largest number ever. The census taker had to ask, for example, whether the origin of each homeless child was "respectable"; whether each pauper was "habitually intemperate"; and whether there were any idiots in the family, and if so, whether their heads were larger or smaller than average.

Through the 19th century, groups that compiled the census were disbanded each time after publication of the results. Census takers had been U.S. marshals and those appointed by them. In 1902, Congress recognized the need for continuity in the census work and set up a permanent office which became the Census Bureau within the Department of Interior. The office was transferred in the following year to the Department of Commerce and Labor. When Commerce and Labor split into separate departments in 1913, the bureau remained with Commerce, where it still is.

Congress continued until 1930 to write census questions. Now the responsibility rests with the bureau itself, although in recent years individual lawmakers have tried to limit the number and scope of census questions. A census of housing has been combined with the census of population since 1940. Computers were used for the first time in 1950 for tabulating and analyzing census statistics, which by then had become almost too voluminous to handle manually. In addition to the decennial census of population and housing, the Census Bureau conducts censuses of manufacturing, business, mineral industries, and state and local government finances in years ending in 2 and 7 and a census of agriculture in years ending in 4 and 9.

Importance to New Deal and Redistricting

Despite its permanent status, the Census Bureau enjoyed little support or funding from Congress and degenerated into a "statistical factory" during the first part of this century, Scott wrote in her history. The bureau regained some prestige during Hoover's presidency. At his suggestion, it began to provide information for the Commerce Department's monthly publication *Survey of Current Business*. But it was the Depression, and more specifically the New Deal, that put new life in the bureau. "The importance of statistics increased dramatically as the flood of social and economic legislation brought unprecedented demands for accurate, up-to-date information. . . ."[21]

World War II brought an even greater demand for census information, and during the war years the bureau first developed

---

[21] *Ibid.*, p. 42.

Censuses, 1790-1980

Date	Population	Percent Increase
1790 (Aug. 2)	3,929,214	—
1800 (Aug. 4)	5,308,483	35.1
1810 (Aug. 6)	7,239,881	36.4
1820 (Aug. 7)	9,638,453	33.1
1830 (June 1)	12,866,020	33.5
1840 (June 1)	17,069,453	32.7
1850 (June 1)	23,191,876	35.9
1860 (June 1)	31,443,321	35.6
1870 (June 1)	39,818,449	26.6
1880 (June 1)	50,155,783	26.0
1890 (June 1)	62,947,714	25.5
1900 (June 1)	75,994,575	20.7
1910 (Apr. 15)	91,972,266	21.0
1920 (Jan. 1)	105,710,620	14.9
1930 (Apr. 1)	122,775,046	16.1
1940 (Apr. 1)	131,669,275	7.2
1950 (Apr. 1)	150,697,361	14.5
1960 (Apr. 1)	179,323,175	18.5
1970 (Apr. 1)	203,235,000	13.3
*1980 (Apr. 1)	221,700,000	9.0

* Estimate

scientifically valid techniques of sampling small segments of the population to discern trends for the entire population. After the war, Congress once again lost interest in the bureau. Funds were reduced and hundreds of bureau employees lost their jobs. But the Commerce Department sponsored a study of the Census Bureau, drawing testimony from experts in many fields, which persuaded Congress to rethink its attitude. "The benchmark census records are essential to current and prospective action programs," the study concluded. "Without them it would not be possible to analyze probable consequences of proposed action."[22] With the New Frontier and Great Society social programs, the Census Bureau regained some of the vitality of the New Deal years.

Another development also cast public attention on the importance of reliable, accurate and complete censuses. The 1960 census revealed the extent of legislative malapportionment. In Michigan, the 16th congressional district had a population of 802,994 and the 12th district only 177,431. In 21 states, at least one congressional district was twice as populous as another. By 1964, fewer than 40 percent of the voters in 39 of the 50 states could elect a majority of the members of both houses of Congress.

[22] "Appraisal of the Census Programs," Report of the Intensive Review Committee to the Secretary of Commerce, February 1954.

These statistical pictures fortified arguments for reapportionment and paved the way for the "one man-one vote" decisions of the Supreme Court. It ruled that congressional districts should be about equal in population, and later extended that ruling to state legislative districts.[23] Robert G. Dixon Jr., a political scientist, wrote: "In the space of five years reapportionment virtually remade the political map of America. . . . By the election of 1966, the equal population rule had affected virtually every legislative seat and congressional district in the nation . . . and had reconstituted a fair number of city council and county board seats as well."[24]

The Supreme Court in 1970 extended the "one-man one-vote" rule, holding that it applied to any election — state or local — of persons to perform governmental functions. When members of local administrative boards, such as school boards, are elected by ward or district, those districts must be equal in populations "as far as practicable."[25]

Demographic Change and Analysis

A BOVE ALL, the decennial census is the nation's measuring rod of population growth and demographic change. If the 1980 count measures up to Census Bureau projections, it will show 221.7 million people living in the 50 states and the District of Columbia, some 18.5 million more than a decade earlier. This 10-year increase would thus be the smallest since the 1930s.

But that is no surprise to demographers who have watched the downward trend in childbearing since 1958, the year the postwar "baby boom" began to taper off and ultimately become the "baby bust." The year 1980 will be the peak year in the 18-24 age group (29.5 million). While the size of this group will begin to shrink, the 65-and-older segment of the population will continue to grow progressively faster before it, too, levels off in the next decade. But this will only be a pause for the older group. Much swifter growth lies ahead.[26]

It is also no surprise that the population is continuing to move westward and southward. The 1980 census is expected to show

---

[23] The court in 1962, in Baker *v.* Carr (369 U.S. 186), accepted jurisdiction in congressional redistricting. In 1964, it laid down the principle of "one man-one vote" in congressional districting in Westberry *v.* Sanders (376 U.S. 1) and in state legislative districts in Reynolds *v.* Sims (377 U.S. 533). See "Reapportionment Struggle," *E.R.R.*, pp. 703-708, and Congressional Quarterly's *Representation and Reapportionment Struggle* (1966), p. 53.
[24] Robert G. Dixon, *Democratic Representation: Reapportionment in Law and Politics* (1968), pp. 3-4.
[25] Hadley *v.* Junior College District of Metropolitan Kansas City, Mo.
[26] See "America in the 1980s," *E.R.R.*, 1979 Vol. II, pp. 868-870.

that the nation's "center of population" has shifted west of the
Mississippi River for the first time. The center of population is
the theoretical point at which the nation would be in balance if
it were perched atop a pole with only the weight of the people
considered. The westward migration is one of the nation's oldest
demographic trends. In 1790, the year of the first decennial census, the center of population was slightly east of Baltimore, and
by 1970 it had moved to Mascoutah, Ill., 30 miles east of the
Mississippi.

Since 1960, and especially during the past decade, the westward movement has been complemented by the growth of the
"Sun Belt." While there is no strict definition of which states
belong to the Sun Belt, it does embrace the southern tier of
states stretching from California to Florida plus some more. The
Population Reference Bureau Inc., a non-profit demographic research center in Washington, D.C., lists 15 states in this category, all characterized by "a mild climate, recreation facilities,
and expanding job opportunities." They are Alabama, Arizona,
Arkansas, California, Florida, Georgia, Louisiana, Missouri,
Mississippi, New Mexico, North Carolina, Oklahoma, South
Carolina, Texas and Virginia.

Those states accounted for about a third of the U.S. population growth in the 1960s. By 1977, according to Census Bureau
estimates, the figure was nearly 40 percent. Florida alone added
more people than the northeastern and north-central states
combined. By the beginning of 1979, the Sun Belt had absorbed
two-thirds of the nation's population growth during the decade.
Florida, Texas and California led the way.[27]

Most of the growth in the South was accounted for by whites,
but beginning in 1975 the flow of blacks moving to the South
had grown as strong as the steadily diminishing wave of depar-
tures.[28] It is not clear whether the majority of blacks moving to
the South are returning home or going to the region for the first
time. The 1980 census may provide the answer to this question.
In general, the South's growth is accounted for by the migration
of non-southerners.[29]

Two other important demographic trends are expected to
show up in the 1980 census. One is a continuance of a long-term
movement to the suburbs despite some reverse migration of
middle-class whites back into the cities. The other is the more
recent "rural renaissance." Richard Scammon, former director

[27] See Jeanne C. Biggar's "The Sunning of America: Migration to the Sunbelt," *Population Bulletin,* publication of the Population Reference Bureau, Inc., March 1979, p. 6.
[28] U.S. Bureau of the Census, "Geographical Mobility: March 1975 to 1978," *Current
Population Reports,* November 1978, p. 1.
[29] Larry H. Long and Kristin A. Hansen, "Trends in Return Migration to the South,"
Demography, Vol. 12, No. 4, November 1975, pp. 601-614.

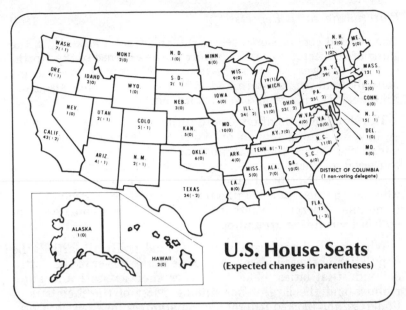

U.S. House Seats
(Expected changes in parentheses)

of the Census Bureau, calls the growth of the suburbs "the most significant social and political" development since World War II, and he predicts the trend will continue "despite rising gasoline and home heating costs."[30] From 1970 to 1977, a time marked by the 1973-74 gasoline shortages, the suburban population increased by 12.3 percent, the Census Bureau estimates.

Beyond the suburbs, in non-metropolitan areas, growth was first noted in the 1960s. And in the 1970s — for the first time in this century — population growth was higher in non-metropolitan than metropolitan areas. Part of the rural regeneration came from "urban sprawl" into neighboring counties from metropolitan areas, but a large portion resulted from the growth of retirement communities, especially in those parts of the South and West where climates are mild and living costs are low.[31]

Expected Gains and Losses of House Seats

Census Bureau projections indicate that the South and West will gain 14 new seats in the House of Representatives as a result of the 1980 census, three seats more than the two regions gained after 1970.[32] Then, as is expected now, they were the only re-

---

[30] Quoted by Gerald Rosen in "Politics: A New Ball Game in the 1980s," *Dun's Review,* January 1980, pp. 42-46.

[31] A report by a congressional committee on population change in the United States concluded, however, that the "rural renaissance" may be only a temporary reaction to current economic problems. See "Domestic Consequences of United States Population Change," Select Committee on Population, U.S. House of Representatives, December 1978. For further background, see "Rural Migration," *E.R.R.,* 1975 Vol. II, pp. 581-600.

[32] The Census Bureau predicted before the 1970 census that it would result in the shift of nine House seats. The actual figure was 11. The bureau correctly named the states (Arizona, California, Colorado, Florida and Texas) that would gain, but it underestimated the number California and Florida would add. California added five rather than four seats, and Florida added three rather than two. The other three states received one each, as predicted.

gions to add congressional seats. But this time, unlike 1970, the gains are expected to come entirely at the expense of the Northeast and Midwest *(see map)*. After the 1970 census, losses came not only from northeastern and midwestern states but also from Alabama, Tennessee and West Virginia.

The shifts in population — and ultimately congressional seats — have intriguing though by no means clear-cut political implications. Areas that are growing fastest tend to be more conservative than those losing population, especially the big cities of the Northeast and Midwest. What is not clear is whether the newcomers influence conservative bastions to become more liberal or whether they themselves become less liberal in their new surroundings.[33]

Whatever the implications for national political parties, the population changes indicate a decline in the power of the northern industrial cities, older industries such as steel and automobiles and the large labor unions. Most of the members of Congress who backed federal loan guarantees for Chrysler Corp. were from the industrial North.[34] Had the vote occurred after the 1980 census, it might have been different. On the other hand, the Sun Belt industries — aerospace, energy, agriculture, textiles and tourism — may get a boost.

Mid-Decade Censuses Beginning in 1985

One of the clearest messages of current population statistics is that Americans are on the move. About 36 million persons — one of every six Americans — move in a typical year. Thus decennial census figures quickly become obsolete. The Census Bureau has developed a series of "intercensal" estimates to keep up with the changing population, but beginning in 1985 it will conduct mid-decade censuses. Congress began studying the idea of a mid-decade census in 1962, but little headway was made until 1976, largely because of cost factors. However, as specialized updating of census statistics grew more expensive, the price tag on a mid-decade count seemed less formidable.

Congress finally approved the mid-decade census in October 1976. Though the first one is scheduled for 1985, no one is sure exactly what form it will take. As costs have soared, the idea of conducting a full-scale head count has been abandoned. More likely, the 1985 census will be based on a survey of households, using sampling methods perfected over the years. The information would not affect congressional apportionment, but it would

---

[33] New England political analysts ascribe a liberal bent in parts of southern New Hampshire, traditionally a conservative state, to former Boston area residents who moved across the state line. However, it is noted that jobs or lower taxes, rather than retirement, attracted those persons. Conservatism runs high in retirement communities, even if the people came from areas considered politically liberal.

[34] See *Congressional Quarterly Weekly Report*, Dec. 29, 1979, pp. 2968-2969.

The Demographic Business

The corporate demand for demographic information — on where to locate a factory, movie theater or shopping center — has spawned a new business. Reid Reynolds, senior editor of *American Demographics* magazine counts about 30 companies that have sprung up to supply this demand. Only a few of them were in existence a decade ago. In fact his magazine is new, reporting on demographic activity of various kinds.

The Census Bureau is the primary source of information for such demographic specialization. In 1970, the bureau for the first time placed census information on relatively inexpensive computer tapes. Since census information is in the public domain, it may be used by anyone.

be used to allocate federal funds and for federal and local government planning.

Some demographers and other social scientists have questioned whether traditional head counts should be conducted at all — even for the decennial censuses. Given the likelihood of a large undercount no matter how much the Census Bureau tries to improve its methods, some people believe a large-scale sampling program would be more effective in sketching the nation's profile — and much cheaper as well. Andrew Hacker, a political scientist at Queens College in New York City, contends that the Census Bureau has developed the capability of providing an accurate look at the nation, down to the smallest detail, without the massive head counts. "They can judge not only the populations of states and cities, but how many teenagers there are in a given rural county. It is also possible to provide trustworthy data for small tracts of territory to serve as jigsaw puzzle pieces when legislative districts are drawn."[35]

Census officials are reluctant to abandon a full-scale count, especially one which has become so important to many sectors of society. They point out that it is the Constitution — not the Census Bureau — that requires the decennial head counts. And although they acknowledge the accuracy of the bureau's methods for estimating population and other demographic characteristics, many feel the full enumeration is needed as a "benchmark" on which to base later estimates.

The Population Reference Bureau thinks the 1980 census "will measure some of the most dramatic changes in our nation's history" and that it will be the "most closely observed in U.S. history since the first census of 1790." In 1980, the American people, it seems, will be watching the census just as carefully as it is watching them. What happens this time, may decide what future censuses will be like.

[35] See Andrew Hacker's "The No-Account Census," *Harper's*, March 1980, p. 31.

119

Selected Bibliography

Books

Callahan, Daniel, ed., *The American Population Debate,* Doubleday & Co. 1971.

Congressional Districts in the 1970s," Congressional Quarterly Inc., 1974 (2nd ed.)

Dixon, Robert G., *Democratic Representation; Reapportionment in Law and Politics,* Oxford University Press, 1968.

Scott, Ann Herbert, *Census, U.S.A.,* Seabury Press, 1968.

Sundquist, James L., *Dispersing Population: What America Can Learn from Europe,* The Brookings Institution, 1975.

Articles

Carson, Gerald, "The Great Enumeration," *American Heritage,* December 1979.

Hardesty, Rex, "Politics in the 1980s: The Census Redraws the Lines," *AFL-CIO Federationist,* November 1979.

Herriot, Roger A., "The 1980 Census: The Countdown for a Complete Count," *Monthly Labor Review,* September 1979.

"Reapportionment and Minorities," *Focus,* December 1979.

Robey, Bryant, "The Statistical Nightmare (Adjusting for the Census Undercount)," *American Demographics,* February 1980.

Rosen, Gerald, "Politics: A Whole New Ball Game in the 1980s," *Dun's Review,* January 1980.

Reports and Studies

Biggar, Jeanne C., "The Sunning of America: Migration to the Sunbelt," *Population Bulletin,* The Population Reference Bureau Inc., Vol. 34, No. 1, March 1979.

Francese, Peter K., "The 1980 Census: The Counting of America," *Population Bulletin,* The Population Reference Bureau Inc., Vol. 34, No. 4, September 1979.

National Academy of Sciences, "Counting the People in 1980: An Appraisal of Census Plans," 1978.

U.S. Department of Commerce, Bureau of the Census, "Population Profile of the United States: 1978," Current Population Report, April 1979.

U.S. General Accounting Office, "Bureau of the Census Planning, Budgeting, and Accounting for the 1980 Census," Dec. 12, 1978.

——"Programs to Reduce the Decennial Census Undercount," May 5, 1976.

Editorial Research Reports, "Census Taking, 1970," 1970 Vol. I, p. 203; "Population Profile of the United States," 1967 Vol. II, pp. 801; "Reapportionment Struggle," 1964 Vol. II, p. 701.

FREEDOM OF INFORMATION ACT: A REAPPRAISAL

by

William V. Thomas

Feb. 16
1 9 7 9

(**Report update:** In a ruling seen by many as a weakening of the Freedom of Information Act, the Supreme Court on March 3, 1980, held that written data produced and possessed by a private organization conducting federally funded studies are not federal records and therefore not subject to disclosure under the act. The case was *Forsham v. Harris.*)

FREEDOM OF INFORMATION ACT: A REAPPRAISAL

O F ALL the "rights" Americans enjoy, perhaps the most difficult to define or legislate is "the right to know." The Freedom of Information Act (FOIA), signed into law in 1966, was designed to make federal agencies disclose more information to the public.[1] Since its enactment, tens of thousands of previously secret files have been opened to citizen view. The statute has helped shed light on such diverse subjects as the CIA's mind control experiments and the espionage conviction of Julius and Ethel Rosenberg.[2] But despite its use in uncovering cases of possible wrongdoing by public officials, many believe that the Freedom of Information Act is still a long way from accomplishing its goal of ending government behind closed doors.

Access to information is limited by the very nature of the government's data-gathering network. The growth of the federal bureaucracy, the proliferation of agencies, and the increasing volume of paperwork all pose formidible barriers to compliance with the law.[3] The sheer number of requests for information — estimates put the figure at around 150,000 a year since 1975 — makes prompt response difficult.

The Freedom of Information Act states that all records in the possession of the executive branch of the federal government must be provided to anyone on request, unless they are specifically exempted from disclosure by the law. There are nine categories of information that are exempted from public disclosure (see p. 131). But according to Martin Michaelson, a Washington, D.C., public interest lawyer, the exemptions are "broad enough to protect massive amounts of secrets."[4] Some agencies, particularly those involved in national security, intelligence and law enforcement, routinely deny citizens access to their files; others that do respond to requests often deliver incomplete or heavily censored data.

---

[1] The FOIA applies only to the administrative agencies of the executive branch of the federal government. It does not apply to Congress or the judiciary.
[2] The Rosenbergs were convicted in 1950 of passing atomic secrets to Russia, and three years later, put to death after a protracted and celebrated case.
[3] See "America's Information Boom," *E.R.R.*, 1978 Vol. II, pp. 801-820.
[4] Martin Michaelson, "Freedom of Information: Up Against the Stone Wall," *The Nation*, May 15, 1977, p. 625.

From the outset, the Freedom of Information Act was unpopular with executive branch officials. Presidents Nixon and Ford both were accused of slowing down congressional efforts to strengthen requirements of the law. Ford in 1974 vetoed a bill embodying stiffer disclosure provisions for the original FOIA, but his veto was overridden *(see p. 132)*. So far, the Carter administration appears willing to support broader access to government files. In 1977, Attorney General Griffin B. Bell issued guidelines requiring federal agencies to divulge information as long as its release would not be demonstrably harmful to the government or the individual concerned.

In March, Congress is expected to begin hearings on new charters for the CIA and the FBI *(see p. 136)*. The deliberations will center on the question of how much information individuals have a right to know and how much the government needs to keep secret. Sen. Birch Bayh, D-Ind., chairman of the Senate Intelligence Committee, described the tension between the competing interests. "The intelligence agencies of the United States are vital to the success of this country's foreign and military policies," Bayh said. "But these agencies . . . always will be a potential threat to the rights of Americans, because they operate in secret and . . . have massive information-gathering capabilities. At stake [in the hearings] are fundamental constitutional rights of speech, press, assembly and privacy."[5]

Complaints of Law Enforcement Agencies

The General Accounting Office reported in November that law enforcement authorities and other officials "at all levels of government" have complained "that the proliferation of access laws has been instrumental in creating a restrictive climate which affects their ability to obtain information from the public and institutions, to recruit and maintain informants and to exchange information with other agencies."[6] Law enforcement agencies in particular complain that they are overwhelmed by information requests from individuals, the press and public interest groups. The only people who are satisfied with the "present mess," according to one official in the Office of Management and Budget, are lawyers helping clients make use of the federal law.

The Justice Department reported that it spent over 500,000 man-hours in 1977 answering requests for information. "We are now committed to the maximum practical release of departmental records," said Assistant Attorney General Benjamin R.

---

[5] Speaking before the U.S. Senate, Jan. 25, 1978.

[6] U.S. General Accounting Office, "Impact of the Freedom of Information and Privacy Acts on Law Enforcement Agencies," Nov. 15, 1978, p. 1.

Common Cause Openness Rankings

Ranking	Agency	Score*
1	Export-Import Bank	0.0
2	National Labor Relations Board	10.2
3	Occupational Safety and Health Review Commission	11.5
4	United States Parole Commission	16.2
5	Federal Reserve Board	18.9
6	Commodity Futures Trading Commission	26.0
7	Federal Home Loan Bank Board	28.8
8	Federal Deposit Insurance Corporation	28.9
9	Postal Rate Commission	33.3
10	Federal Election Commission	36.8
11	Securities and Exchange Commission	37.8
12	Federal Trade Commission	43.2
13	Equal Employment Opportunity Commission	43.5
14	Federal Maritime Commission	58.2
15	United States Commission on Civil Rights	61.7
16	Federal Communications Commision	62.6
17	Renegotiation Board	62.7
18	Nuclear Regulatory Commission	64.3
19	Consumer Product Safety Commission	73.7
20	United States International Trade Commission	77.5
21	National Transportation Safety Board	80.8
22	Civil Aeronautics Board	84.1
23	Federal Energy Regulatory Commission	88.8
24	Indian Claims Commission	88.8
25	Interstate Commerce Commission	90.4
26	Tennessee Valley Authority	100.0

* Survey covered most active agencies from March 1977 to March 1978. Rankings based on percentage of meetings open to the public.

Civiletti. "But we cannot accept the proposition that continued expenditures of resources [to meet FOIA requirements] are appropriate when weighed against the other important missions of the department."[7]

Many public interest groups regard the Justice Department and the FBI as the most uncooperative agencies in government when it comes to responding to information requests. In order to improve its response time, the FBI in 1977 brought hundreds of field agents to Washington to help reduce its backlog of inquiries. But the bureau has said that part of the reason why it delays and often denies public access to its files is accounted for by the kind of data it collects — criminal information it regards as too important to be released in haste.

---

[7] Quoted in *The New York Times*, Aug. 8, 1977.

Federal law enforcement officials believe that many requests for information come from prisoners and lawbreakers. The Drug Enforcement Agency has estimated that about 40 percent of its inquiries are from prisoners asking not only for their own files but also for sensitive data, including agents' manuals and laboratory reports describing the manufacture of dangerous drugs.[8] FBI Director William H. Webster said recently that the Freedom of Information Act also is being used by figures in organized crime to try to gain access to investigative files.

Congress has moved with deliberate caution on many of the problems surrounding the FOIA provisions and their application. One stumbling block for lawmakers has been the difficulty in getting information on how the act actually is operating. Some agencies and departments have been lax in reporting information on the number of requests for data, as required by law. Legal experts believe that the act could be improved by (1) requiring more detailed recordkeeping on compliance, (2) further defining the court's authority to enjoin release of requested information, and (3) rewriting the exemption for law enforcement agencies to prevent them from blocking access to their files.

Media Use of Access Rights Under FOIA

As soon as amendments to the Freedom of Information Act took effect, in February 1975, reporters began besieging government agencies with requests for data. Within a year after the amendments' passage, Jack Taylor of the *Daily Oklahoman* obtained a copy of the Army Department's study on the 1968 My Lai massacre in Vietnam; the Associated Press gained information with which to put together a list of high-level regulatory agency officials who had worked for the industries they regulated; and *The Washington Star* discovered that the CIA was training local police departments in intelligence-gathering techniques.

Despite some notable successes, journalists continue to report delays and footdragging by agencies reluctant to make certain requested data public. The FOIA amendments stipulated that fees charged by an agency for searching through its records should be waived when the release of documents is in the public interest. But David Vladeck of the Freedom of Information Clearinghouse, a Washington-based Ralph Nader project, said that federal offices frequently "overlook" that requirement. Agencies still use high fees as a way of discouraging scholars and newspaper writers, Vladeck said. The Nader organization has

---

[8] "Impact of the Freedom of Information and Privacy Acts on Law Enforcement Agencies," *op. cit.,* p. 3.

gone to court a number of times to have such fees lowered or eliminated. In spite of these problems, the FOIA regulations are "working well," Vladeck said. Any regulations are "obviously going to encounter some resistance," he added. "But the good points of the Freedom of Information Act far outweigh a few lingering difficulties."

Public interest groups have charged that some news agencies themselves may be responsible for withholding information from the public. "Invoking 'news judgment' and pleading time and space limitations, news-media managers [pose] an inevitable bottleneck in the flow of information," wrote Prof. Richard A. Schwarzlose of Northwestern University. "One need only to think of the multiplication of information that has so affected the social and physical sciences, as well as policymaking, in recent years to realize how little the media have expanded time, space or depth to accommodate the expansion."[9]

Protection of Data by the Privacy Act

One problem in affording increased public access to information has been providing adequate protection for individual rights to privacy. Concerned that the information gathering and dispensing activities of the federal government had "expanded to such an extent that they are becoming a threat to the constitutionally protected right of privacy," Congress enacted the Privacy Act of 1974.[10] The act applied to all federal agencies that maintain a system of records containing personal information about individuals, although law enforcement agencies were exempted from certain provisions of the law.[11]

The legislation adopted a dual approach to protecting individual privacy from government encroachment. It called on government to police itself, requiring agencies to limit their recordkeeping activities and to prevent disclosure of information, except under special circumstances. In addition, the law set up procedures under which individual citizens could gain access to their records and challenge those that were inaccurate.

The Carter administration is planning to ask Congress to enact even stricter legislation to curb the amount of information on the private lives of Americans that now flows through the computers of businesses and law enforcement agencies. Rec-

---

[9] Richard A. Schwarzlose, "For Journalists Only," *Columbia Journalism Review*, July-August 1977, p. 33.

[10] See "Rights to Privacy" *E.R.R.*, 1974 Vol. II, pp. 785-804.

[11] In 1974, Congress moved to clarify student rights when it passed the Family Education Rights and Privacy Act. Known as the Buckley Amendment, for its sponsor Sen. James L. Buckley, Cons. R-N.Y., the bill required educational institutions to permit parents and students over 18 to inspect the student's files and records and, in most cases, to obtain their consent before releasing information to a third party.

ommendations contained in a 207-page White House memorandum recently obtained by *The New York Times* cover the protection of medical files, personal financial and insurance records and certain legal data.[12] The central points in the memorandum are expected to serve as the foundation of Carter's special message on privacy, which he will deliver to Congress sometime this spring.

The White House memorandum included proposals to (1) require insurance companies to inform their clients of company data disclosure practices, (2) forbid the release of personal information by any private company "where there is an expectation of confidentiality," and (3) establish procedures whereby individuals can challenge the accuracy of non-government records. Although Carter has not spoken publicly on specific issues in the memorandum, the Department of Health, Education and Welfare has begun drafting legislation to increase safeguards on private medical files.

Origin of Citizen Access Rights

THE FOUNDING FATHERS recognized the connection between democratic government and an informed populace. George Washington, who suffered more than his share of criticism from the press, believed in the importance of the free exchange of ideas in a democracy. He once wrote that the process was necessary so "citizens at large may be well informed, and decide, with respect to public measures, upon a thorough knowledge of the facts. Concealment is a species of misinformation."[13]

The First Amendment to the Constitution states: "Congress shall make no law respecting an establishment of religion, or prohibiting the full exercise thereof; or abridging the freedom of speech, or the press; or the right of the people peaceably to assemble, and to petition the government for redress of grievances." The long-cherished American "right to know" is rooted in those words. History offers a guide to their origins but not to their precise meaning, since that is largely a matter of the Supreme Court's continuing interpretation.

Historians find seeds of the First Amendment in the 18th century Enlightenment. Philosophers of that period stressed the

---

[12] *The New York Times,* Dec. 29, 1978.
[13] Quoted by James E. Pollard, *The Presidents and the Press* (1947), pp. 29-30.

divinity of reason and the rights of the individual. In particular, they held freedom of inquiry to be not only an inherent human right but basic to the advancement of knowledge and the discovery of truth. This underlying principle of the Enlightenment was later reflected in the American political philosophy of popular sovereignty and democratic rule.

The Founding Fathers believed that in order to judge the propriety of a state's actions, the citizenry must have information about the activities of government. "This is the reason for . . . freedom of the press," historian Henry Steele Commager has written. "This was the logic behind Jefferson's famous statement that given a choice between government without newspapers and newspapers without government he would choose the latter; this was the philosophy that animated that passion for education expressed by most of the Constitution makers: that without enlightenment about politics and information about government, democracy simply would not work."[14] On the other hand, Commager continued, "the Constitution itself was drawn up in secret session." Clearly, the Founding Fathers had inconsistent attitudes about government secrecy.

Government Suppression of News in War

One of the principal sources of information about the goings-on in government is the press. American history is replete with struggles between governmental institutions and the fourth estate over the release of data deemed to be in the public interest. Acceptance of the principle of freedom of information has never brought tranquility to the relations between newspapers and politicians.

The Federalist Party attempted to silence press opposition to its policies through the Sedition Act of 1798. Even before the act was passed, the Federalists moved against Benjamin Franklin Bache, a Philadelphia printer who was one of their most persistent critics. In 1795 a U.S. senator turned over to Bache a copy of the Jay Treaty with Great Britain, which the Senate had voted to keep secret.[15] Bache published the full text of the document and set off a public protest that the administration was sacrificing national interests to the recent oppressor of the American colonists.

Bache again embarrassed the Federalists in 1798, at the time of America's undeclared naval war with France. In an attempt to avert an all-out war, he published correspondence between

---

[14] Henry Steele Commager, writing in *The New York Review of Books*, Aug. 19, 1973.
[15] The treaty was designed to settle difficulties arising mainly out of violations of the Treaty of Paris of 1793 and to regulate commerce and navigation.

the French government and American envoys in Paris which indicated a conciliatory attitude on the part of France. The Federalists brought a common-law prosecution for seditious libel against Bache in June of 1798 and cited his actions as justification for the Sedition Act, which was signed into law the following month. Among other things, the act made it a crime, punishable by up to two years' imprisonment and $2,000 in fines, to speak or publish any "false, scandalous and malicious" statement against the government or its high officials with "intent to defame them."[16]

The Civil War resulted in direct military censorship for the first time in the nation's history. Union armies censored the dispatches of several correspondents in an attempt — never entirely successful — to keep Confederate spies from learning from northern newspapers about battle plans and army movements. News suppression in the Civil War sometimes extended to matters of opinion as well as security. The Postmaster General barred from the mails several northern periodicals opposed to the war. And on occasion editors were sent to jail on orders of the Secretary of War or Secretary of State.

During the two world wars, the press and the government cooperated in withholding sensitive information from the public. In April 1917, President Wilson established the Committee on Public Information as an agency of "censorship and publicity." For the guidance of newspapers, the CPI listed 18 specific types of information, such as troop and ship movements, the location of coastal defenses, and items relating to military experiments, which "obviously must not be mentioned in print." And it advised editors that "matters of doubtful nature ...should not be given publicity until submitted to and passed by the committee."

The Office of Censorship, created Dec. 19, 1941, by President Roosevelt, was the World War II version of the CPI. Between Jan. 15, 1942, and May 15, 1945, it issued five editions of its press and broadcasting codes. The codes described various types of information which should not be published or broadcast "except when made available officially by appropriate authority." Supplementing the general codes from time to time were special requests to observe caution with regard to particular subjects, such as trips of the president, the forthcoming invasion of France, research in atomic energy, and the like. Government censorship of the media was ended on Aug. 15, 1945, the day after Japan surrendered.

---

[16] See *The Annals of America*, Vol. IV (published by the Encyclopedia Britannica, 1968), pp. 53-58. Bache died before he could be brought to trial for violating the Sedition Act.

During the 1950s members of the press joined in a campaign to make federal agencies release more information to the public. At the time disclosure of information by agencies of the executive branch was governed by Section 3 of the Administrative Procedure Act of 1946. Since its enactment Section 3 had been criticized for vagueness and bills to tighten its requirements were introduced in every Congress until 1966.

Congressional Efforts Leading to FOIA

In 1955 the House of Representatives established a Foreign Operations and Government Information Subcommittee, under the chairmanship of John E. Moss, D-Calif., to carry out periodic investigations of government information procedures. Moss became a leading proponent of a more liberal law. Moss's efforts were supported by the press, the American Civil Liberties Union, the American Bar Association and some legal scholars, all of whom contended that existing law was being used inconsistently by agencies, often as an excuse to withhold information to which the public had a right.

After more than a decade of debate, Congress in 1966 passed the Freedom of Information Act. Like the 1946 statute, the new law required agencies to publish procedures and rules in the Federal Register, to make publicly available all final opinions, statements of policy and staff manuals, and to maintain an index of these. However, where the 1946 law had permitted agencies at their discretion to exempt from this rule material "required for good cause to be held confidential," the Freedom of Information Act permitted exemption only of materials which met one or more of nine specific requirements:

1. "Specifically required by executive order to be kept secret in the interest of the national defense or foreign policy."

2. Related "solely" to agencies' internal personnel rules and practices.

3. Specifically exempted from disclosure by statute.

4. Privileged or confidential trade secrets or financial information.

5. Inter- or intra-agency memoranda or letters which would be unavailable by law to a person in litigation with the agency.

6. Personnel and medical files "the disclosure of which would constitute a clearly unwarranted invasion of personal privacy."

7. Investigatory files compiled for law enforcement purposes except to the extent available by law to private parties.

8. Contained in or related to examination or condition reports of agencies regulating financial institutions.

9. Geological and geophysical information and data, including maps, concerning wells.[17]

ʲ The Freedom of Information Act was opposed by the agencies it affected and, to some extent, by business interests. The nine exemptions to the disclosure rule were designed to overcome the principal objections while preserving the public's right of access to government information. But critics of the act charged that the exemptions allowed the government to keep secret almost as much material as before.

Studies of the operation of the law noted that the primary problems in obtaining information were bureaucratic delay, the cost of bringing suit to force disclosure, and excessive charges levied by the agencies for finding and providing the requested information. The limitations of the law were dramatized by the slow pace of lawsuits brought against government agencies that refused to release requested documents and records. For example, only eight FOIA cases were decided by the courts in 1970, 20 in 1971, 28 in 1972 and 16 in 1973.[18]

The Supreme Court highlighted another problem in 1973 when it ruled[19] that Congress in the 1966 law had not given the courts the power to remove a "classified" label from information sought by a citizen under the Freedom of Information Act. If the information was classified it was exempt from release, the court maintained.

To deal with these problems, Congress in 1974 amended the Freedom of Information Act to make it easier, quicker and less expensive to get government information. Among other things, the amendments (1) directed each agency to publish a uniform set of fees for providing documents at the cost of finding and copying them, (2) empowered federal district courts to order agencies to produce improperly withheld documents and to examine the contested materials privately to determine if they were properly exempted under one of the nine categories, (3) set time limits for agency responses to requests,[20] (4) set a 30-day time limit for an agency response to a complaint filed in court under the act, (5) allowed courts to order the government to pay attorneys' fees and court costs for persons winning suits against it under the act, (6) required an annual report to Congress

---

[17] This referred to reports based on explorations by private gas and oil companies.

[18] See Michaelson, *op. cit.,* p. 626.

[19] *Environmental Protection Agency v. Mink,* 410 U.S. 73.

[20] The amendments set a limit of 10 working days for an initial request; 20 working days for an appeal from an initial refusal to produce documents. They also provided for a possible 10 working-day extension which could be granted only once in a single case.

including a list of all agency decisions to withhold information requested under the act, the reasons, the appeals, and the results, and (7) required an annual report from the Attorney General to Congress listing the number of cases arising under the act, the exemption involved in each, the disposition, costs, fees and penalties of each.

The 1974 amendments also removed some of the restrictions on the kinds of information that could be obtained. For example, Congress amended the wording of the national defense and national security exemption to make clear that it applied only to properly classified information, clarifying its intent to allow review of the decision to stamp something "classified."

Recent Abuses of Executive Privilege

Controversy over the Pentagon Papers and Watergate during the Nixon administration brought the problem of government secrecy into sharp focus. At issue in the Pentagon Papers case was the publication by *The New York Times, The Washington Post* and several other newspapers, of excerpts from the 7,000-page *History of the United States Decision-Making Process on Vietnam Policy,* commissioned in 1967 by Robert S. McNamara when he was Secretary of Defense. The study was classified "top secret-sensitive" and consisted of a critique of U.S. Indochina policy up to 1968, plus texts of relevant documents.

Nixon administration officials contended that disclosure of the documents was not only unauthorized but also harmful to the defense and diplomatic interests of the United States. Press executives generally took the position that the study dealt with events long past and thus constituted an historical treatise which the public was entitled to read. The information that appeared in print, they further asserted, was not damaging to national interests; at most, it was embarrassing to those involved in making Vietnam policy.[21]

Although the press won its battle to continue printing portions of the Pentagon Papers, the controversy over government secrecy continued. Later in the Nixon administration, the Watergate scandal drove home dramatically the extent to which the government kept its foreign and domestic operations secret. Subsequent congressional investigations exposed deception and wrongdoing at the highest levels of government, findings that eventually led to Nixon's resignation from the presidency in August 1974. The Watergate scandal helped arouse public indignation over the whole question of government in the shadows.

---

[21] See "Secrecy in Government," *E.R.R.*, 1971 Vol. II, pp. 628-650.

Approach to Unsolved Problems

O BTAINING federal records under the Freedom of Information Act often means navigating a sea of paperwork — a frustration citizens seeking all kinds of government information have come to know first-hand. "On the surface, [paperwork] resembles other noxious byproducts we generate in the course of making things and rendering services we are eager to have," wrote Herbert Kaufman of the Brookings Institution. "More of what we want means more of what we don't want as well."[22]

Economists James T. Bennett and Manuel H. Johnson have their own theory about the bureaucracy's penchant for paperwork. "Unlike private industry in which individuals are promoted and rewarded for reducing costs and increasing efficiency, the bureaucrat is rewarded for expanding the size and scope of government...," they wrote. "Not only are there benefits to the bureaucrat for instituting paperwork, but there are also powerful constituencies created by the paperwork burden and accompanying complex forms and regulations."[23]

The Federal Commission on Paperwork was established in 1976 by President Ford to study ways to eliminate bureaucratic barriers in the government's information network. In its final report, issued in January 1978, the commission recommended a "less is more" approach to the deluge of government reports and documents. The major thrust of the commission's findings was that Washington policymakers should take into account all of the costs of paperwork — including citizen frustration and administrative inefficiencies — as well as the substantial expense in dollars. Private and public sectors spend more than $100 billion a year on paperwork, or about $500 per citizen, the commission estimated.[24]

The commission recommended that federal forms be consolidated and that each agency use existing data whenever possible — including that collected by other agencies — instead of making redundant surveys and/or issuing repetitive forms. Other key recommendations included: (1) creating a Cabinet-level Department of Administration to coordinate the flow of federal information and to facilitate public access to data; (2)

---

[22] Herbert Kaufman, *Red Tape: Its Origins, Uses and Abuses* (1977), p. 60.

[23] James T. Bennett and Manuel H. Johnson, "The Political Economy of Federal Government Paperwork," *Policy Review*, winter 1978, pp. 28, 41.

[24] See U.S. Commission on Federal Paperwork, "Final Summary Report," 1977, p. 5.

creating a government-wide information locating system; (3) simplifying regulations and writing them in easily understood language; and (4) fostering data-sharing among government agencies while establishing more precise statutory definitions of confidentiality.

The commission's recommendations received mixed reviews. The suggestion that a Department of Administration could solve the "information glut" drew particular criticism. "We can encourage each department to tighten up its operations without hiring thousands of more bureaucrats to add to the paperwork," said Rep. Peter H. Kostmayer, D-Pa.[25]

One idea that met with general approval was the proposal to eliminate inconsistent and often conflicting federal information laws and practices. In its final recommendations, the Paperwork Commission urged adoption of criteria for ranking information according to its sensitivity. The most sensitive data would be kept confidential, but only in the face of compelling national interests or to preserve privacy rights. Less sensitive information would be permitted to circulate among agencies, while the least sensitive data would be made available to the public.

In January 1979, Reps. Frank Horton, R-N.Y., Jack Brooks, D-Texas, and Tom Steed, D-Okla., introduced a bill — the Paperwork and Red Tape Reduction Act of 1979 — which provided for establishment of an Office of Federal Information Management Policy in the Office of Management and Budget to oversee all facets of information activities in the federal government. The office would have wide responsibility for setting policy pertaining to federal management activities. The bill also provided for creation of a federal information locator office in the General Services Administration. Hearings on the measure are expected to be held later this year.

National Security and Data Collections

When the Senate Select Intelligence Committee began releasing its report on intelligence community abuses in early 1976, it was enough to startle even the strongest supporters of these government agencies. Americans learned that their government had spied on tens of thousands of fellow citizens, had disrupted political organizations[26] and had engaged in tactics ranging from smear campaigns to force people out of work and efforts to break up marriages, to active involvement in political assassinations.

[25] Testimony before the House Government Operations Subcommittee on Government Information and Individual Rights, Oct. 18, 1977.

[26] The Justice Department in 1976 ordered the FBI to halt its 38-year investigation of the Socialist Workers Party, a small left-wing political group whose complaints about official harassment helped to plunge the bureau into crisis.

The repercussions from those revelations have been felt ever since. Underlying the disclosures in the committee's final report, released in 1977, was the finding that intelligence agencies were operating largely without statutory limitations under loosely regulated policies largely of their own making. The committee recommended that the agencies be placed under the rule of law, a task that has fallen to the present 96th Congress.

Later this month, the new chairman of the Senate Judiciary Committee, Edward M. Kennedy, D-Mass., is expected to introduce a charter limiting the jurisdiction and authority of the FBI's intelligence-gathering activities. Senate Intelligence Committee Chairman Birch Bayh, D-Ind., will introduce a similar charter dealing with foreign intelligence and counterintelligence operations conducted by the FBI, CIA and the National Security Agency. Debates on the charters will provide a classic confrontation between advocates of the rights of individuals to a free and open society and the need to protect citizens and the state from acts of subversion and violence.

FBI Director William H. Webster and Attorney General Griffin B. Bell have acknowledged that public confidence in the FBI has been seriously damaged. Both have sought in testimony before congressional committees to assure the public that they are no longer pursuing political dissidents and "speech crimes" and have reordered their priorities to concentrate on organized and white collar crime, computer fraud, terrorist activities and counterintelligence. "The bureau should not be in the business of gathering information, as distinguished from evidence, to meet the general and unspecified needs of the federal government," Webster stated.[27]

While there is general agreement that FBI domestic security investigations must be based on evidence that a crime has been or is about to be committed, the definition of that criminal standard and the procedures it will entail remain to be resolved. One issue Congress must decide is whether the FBI will be allowed to continue conducting so-called intelligence investigations where the bureau hopes to obtain criminal evidence by pulling together bits and pieces of information about organizations over a long period of time.[28]

Just before the 95th Congress adjourned in October, the Senate passed and President Carter signed into law the Foreign Intelligence Surveillance Act of 1978, restricting the ability of

---

[27] William H. Webster, testifying before the Senate Subcommittee on Administrative Practice and Procedure, Sept. 26, 1978.

[28] See "FBI In Transition," *E.R.R.*, 1977 Vol. II, pp. 721-724.

"Government in the Sunshine"

A four-year campaign by Common Cause and other public interest groups to open government to more public scrutiny was successfully concluded on Sept. 13, 1976, when President Ford signed a law requiring most federal agencies to open their meetings to the public. Called the "Government in the Sunshine Act," it required for the first time that all agencies headed by two or more persons — some 50 of them — conduct their business regularly in public session. The unprecedented open-door requirements embraced regulatory agencies, advisory committees, independent offices, the Postal Service — almost all executive branch agencies except the Cabinet departments.

The legislation barred informal meetings or contacts between agency officials and interested outsiders to discuss pending business. It also required that advance notice be given of the date, place, time and subject of all meetings. Under the law, only meetings dealing with national defense, foreign policy, law enforcement investigations and internal agency matters could be closed.

Opponents complained during congressional hearings on the bill that open meetings would disrupt proceedings, inhibit free discussion and, by presenting just one stage of the decision-making process to the public, create a distorted image of agency procedures. Agency officials also said that permitting affected parties to observe deliberations would subject officials to political pressure. But supporters of sunshine legislation maintained that the experiences of the states — all 50 have some form of "open meeting" statute — had dispelled most such concerns. The long-term benefits, they said, would be clearer public understanding of agency procedures and less distrust of government in general.

This goal still remains elusive. According to a study released by Common Cause in August 1978, many government agencies are following neither the letter nor the spirit of the law. For the period from March 12, 1977, through March 11, 1978, the survey indicated that 36 percent, or 813, of 2,242 meetings held were entirely closed to the public; 26 percent (583) were partially closed; only 38 percent (846) were fully open to the public. As a result of agency reluctance to meet the requirements of the Sunshine Act, the study concluded, the public still knows "little about the workings of most federal agencies."

the executive branch to conduct electronic surveillance in the United States for foreign intelligence purposes. The legislation was the first intelligence agency reform to result from four years of disclosures about illegal and improper intelligence operations. In approving the act, Congress affirmed the right of Americans to be secure from unwarranted invasions of privacy in the United States by domestic intelligence agencies. The lawmakers said, in effect, that the interests of national security do not take

Excessive Surveillance?

"There was . . . no way of knowing whether you were being watched at any given moment," novelist George Orwell wrote of the fictional world he created in *1984*. That infamous date is still five years away, but many Americans seem convinced that Orwell's scenario is dangerously close to reality. Disclosures of massive surveillance of American citizens by the CIA and the FBI often are cited as evidence that Big Brother already is watching everything people do.

One of the most bizarre cases of political surveillance in recent years involved a New Jersey high school student named Lori Paton. In early 1973, Lori, who was then 16, wrote a letter requesting information on the Socialist Labor Party for a paper she was preparing for a social science class. She mistakenly addressed the letter to the Socialist Workers Party, a left-wing organization which was then the subject of an FBI "mail cover" investigation. All mail addressed to the organization was examined by postal authorities and the return addresses recorded and sent to the FBI.

Unbeknownst to her, Lori became the subject of an FBI investigation for possible subversive activities. An agent visited her school to inquire about her and also checked out her family with the local police chief and local credit bureau. Although the investigation turned up no information which discredited Lori or her family, agents in the Newark FBI office entered her name in a "subversives" file. There it would have remained had Lori and her parents not learned about the investigation from school officials who had been questioned. Lori and her teacher filed suit against the FBI and won. In August 1974, a U.S. District Court ordered her file destroyed.

precedence over First and Fourth Amendment Rights but rather are to be constrained by those constitutional provisions.

Effect of Disclosure Laws on Business

With the federal government collecting more business data than ever before, the nation's business community is growing increasingly apprehensive that confidential trade information is being requested and made available through the Freedom of Information Act. Government agencies responsible for handling such information have widely differing rules covering its disclosure. Although FOIA regulations prohibit the release of "trade secrets" and other commercial and financial data, these terms are open to diverse interpretations. Many corporate executives fear that without stronger restrictions, their rivals will be able to obtain valuable competitive advantages by gaining access to certain federal records.

Mark H. Lynch, who pioneered use of the FOIA regulations as an attorney for Ralph Nader's Freedom of Information Clearinghouse, said he has watched the issue very closely. "Although [businessmen] all worry about trade secrets, I don't know of a case where a real secret has been disclosed," he said.[29] Nevertheless, several companies have taken legal steps to prevent the disclosure of trade information. In 1976, the Ashland Oil Company brought suit against the Federal Trade Commission to prevent it from turning over to a congressional committee data obtained "under the promise of confidentiality." A federal appeals court ruled against the oil company, declaring it had not proven that "the materials in the possession of the FTC will necessarily be made public if turned over to Congress."[30]

Despite the court's ruling many businesses are citing what they regard as their right to privacy to keep federal inspectors from securing information in the first place. *The Wall Street Journal* reported recently that a number of corporations are refusing to turn over data on the ground that the Constitution protects them from unreasonable searches and seizures. "We are aggressively doing what we can to protect our constitutional rights," said a spokesman for Burlington Northern, Inc.[31]

As more segments of society begin to exercise what they regard as their privileges under the law, the already blurred distinction between the right to know and the right to be let alone is certain to become even more unclear. Years of legal dispute seem inevitable before the conflicting claims of access and privacy ultimately are resolved.

---

[29] Quoted in *U.S. News & World Report*, Aug. 9, 1976.
[30] *Ashland Oil, Inc. v. FTC.*, 548 F. 2nd 977 (D.C. Cir. 1976).
[31] Quoted in *The Wall Street Journal*, Jan. 22, 1979.

Selected Bibliography

Books

Anuta, Larry D., *Information Game,* Surevelation Press, 1976.
Cox, Arthur M., *The Myths of National Secrecy,* Beacon Press, 1976.
Cross, Harold, *The People's Right to Know,* AMS Press, 1972.
Gilson, Lawrence, *Money and Secrecy: The Citizen's Guide to Reform of State and Federal Policies,* Praeger, 1972.
Hammer, Donald P., ed., *Information Age: Its Development, Its Impact,* Scarecrow Press, 1976.
McHale, John, *The Changing Information Environment,* Westview Press, 1976.
Schmidt, Benno C., *Freedom of the Press vs. Public Access,* Praeger, 1976.
Thurman, David S., *The Right to Access of Information from the Government,* Oceana Press, 1973.
Wise, David, *Politics of Lying: Government Deception, Secrecy and Power,* Random House, 1973.

Articles

"Bureaucracy's Paper Chase," *Time,* Dec. 19, 1977.
Footlick, Jerrold K., "Opening Federal Files," *Newsweek,* June 19, 1978.
"Freedom of Information Producing Many Surprises," *U.S. News & World Report,* Aug. 9, 1976.
Michaelson, Martin, "Freedom of Information: Up Against the Stone Wall," *The Nation,* May 21, 1977.
Relyea, Harold, "The Executive Agencies: Reorganization vs. 'Sunshine,' " *The Nation,* Nov. 27, 1976.
Rosenberg, John, "The FBI Shreds Its Files: Catch in the Information Act," *The Nation,* Feb. 4, 1978.
Rosenthal, Paul C. and Robert S. Grossman, "Congressional Access to Confidential Information Collected by Federal Agencies," *Harvard Journal on Legislation,* December 1977.
" 'Sunshine Act' Gets Clouded Results," *U.S. News & World Report,* July 4, 1977.

Reports and Studies

American Civil Liberties Union, "The New Freedom of Information Act & National Security Information," February 1975; "Your Right to Government Information," January 1975.
Editorial Research Reports, "America's Information Boom," 1978 Vol. II, p. 801; "Secrecy in Government," 1971 Vol. II, p. 627.
General Accounting Office, "Impact of the Freedom of Information and Privacy Acts on Law Enforcement Agencies," Nov. 15, 1978; "Timeliness and Completeness of FBI Responses to Requests Under Freedom of Information and Privacy Acts Have Improved," April 10, 1978.
U.S. Senate Subcommittee on Administrative Practice and Procedure, "Freedom of Information: A Compilation of State Laws," December 1978.

AMERICA'S INFORMATION BOOM

by

William V. Thomas

Nov. 3
1978

AMERICA'S INFORMATION BOOM

HOW MANY electric toothbrushes were sold in the United States last year? What is the current and projected U.S. pet population? How many missiles do the Russians have in Eastern Europe? These questions are typical of the inquiries fueling America's latest high-growth enterprise — the information industry.

Demand for information in the United States is increasing at the rate of 30 percent per year, according to one estimate.[1] That upsurge has been met in part by the publishing trade, which produced over 42,000 books in 1977. Also meeting the challenge are the proliferating number of "information-on-demand" companies that provide their clients with essential, often difficult to obtain, facts and figures. "Without the complex system of indexes, data bases, microforms, directories and other information tools the industry uses, our society would be paralyzed and unable to locate the goods and services it needs," Paul Zurkowski, president of the Information Industry Association, said recently.[2]

In little over a decade, the capabilities of most information-supply companies have expanded considerably. In 1966, according to *Free Enterprise* magazine, there were in this country only 18 computer-assisted data banks whose stores of information could be retrieved and displayed on video terminals or printouts. These 18 data bases, maintained by government agencies and private industries, contained approximately 20,000 items of information. By 1976, the latest year for which statistics are available, there were 360 such data banks, with more than 71 million stored entries.[3]

The production and dissemination of information has replaced manufacturing as the principal activity of the U.S. economy. Information-oriented businesses, ranging from publishing and record keeping to typing, are said to be growing at an annual rate of around 10 percent, or double the rate of growth for the economy as a whole. Part of that growth is accounted for by the hundreds of new companies that sell every conceivable kind of data. Some information-supply organizations generate their own

---

[1] *Free Enterprise* magazine, August 1978, p. 62.
[2] Paul Zurkowski, writing in the *American Library Association Yearbook,* 1978.
[3] See "Reappraisal of Computers," *E.R.R.,* 1971 Vol. I, p. 345-366.

data through direct research. Most, however, are set up to track down the information their customers want. Sometimes that takes only seconds, thanks to computer networks that afford access to stored collections of information throughout the world. [4] One result of the rapid increase in data technology has been a flood of what many see as "useless" information, a phenomena brought about largely by the wide use of photocopy machines.

Companies in the business of supplying information rely to a large extent on the U.S. government and its vast data-producing resources. Some of the information the government produces is secret. The rest theoretically is available to the general public, either free of charge or for a fee. But individual citizens and businesses that need such information often are at a loss to know where to locate the facts they are looking for.

The government frequently sells its information at lower prices than some companies that market the same data. Many information managers in the private sector believe this practice amounts to unfair competition. "The government has the obvious right to compile data," said a publishing executive, "but should not be operating in the marketplace as it does." Industry spokesmen argue that their companies, and not federal agencies, are best equipped to handle the dissemination of most of the data government produces.

Increased Popularity of Newsletters

Contributing to the current information explosion is the mushrooming newsletter business. The exchange of ideas through newsletters is a throwback to the days when members of learned societies circulated observations and reports by mail. Today, there are over 1,500 newsletters published in the United States, conveying specialized information on subjects ranging from gold prices to antique beer cans. Newsletters of from four to 65 pages are printed daily, weekly or monthly, with subscription rates running from $5 to more than $2,000 a year. [5]

For many, newsletters fill the gap between daily newspapers and monthly magazines. "Mass communication is out, personal communication is in. And that's what newsletters are," explained Ray E. Hiebert, dean of the University of Maryland's journalism school. [6] The first American newsletter, the *Whaley-Eaton Letter,* began publication in 1918. Five years later, W.M. Kiplinger started what has become the most successful and influential of all, the *Kiplinger Washington Letter.* The Kiplinger

---

[4] See *Publishers Weekly,* June 7, 1976.
[5] *The Daily Report for Executives,* published by the Bureau of National Affairs in Washington, costs $2,385 a year.
[6] Quoted in *Time,* May 30, 1977.

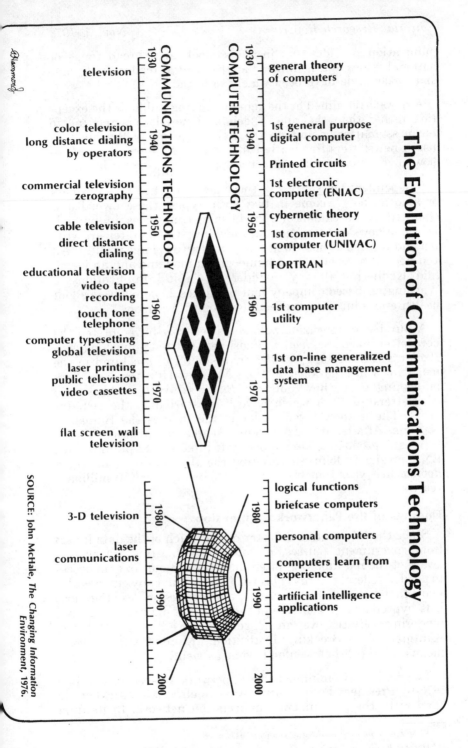

The Evolution of Communications Technology

COMMUNICATIONS TECHNOLOGY

COMPUTER TECHNOLOGY

1930 — television

general theory
of computers

color television
long distance dialing
by operators

1st general purpose
digital computer

Printed circuits

commercial television
zerography

1st electronic
computer (ENIAC)

cybernetic theory

cable television

direct distance
dialing

1st commercial
computer (UNIVAC)

FORTRAN

educational television

video tape
recording

touch tone
telephone

1st computer
utility

computer typesetting
global television

laser printing
public television
video cassettes

1st on-line generalized
data base management
system

flat screen wall
television

logical functions
briefcase computers

3-D television

personal computers

laser
communications

computers learn from
experience

artificial intelligence
applications

SOURCE: John McHale, *The Changing Information Environment*, 1976.

Blummonly

145

publication provides an "insider's" look at a broad range of national issues and is directed at the general reader. Its format and folksy style have been widely imitated.

A newsletter aimed at the general reading public is the exception rather than the rule. Specialized newsletters relating to business matters dominate the field. The many Washington-based newsletters frequently concentrate on "money issues" — how government actions affect a specific industry or business.

Independent newsletters — those not published by a business or association — come in two basic types: those owned and operated by individuals or by publishing companies. Individually owned newsletters require minimal investment, often are written and printed at home and sometimes return large profits. "All you need is a typewriter, a mimeograph machine and an idea," said Kenneth Calloway, founder of Capital Publications, a Washington-based company that publishes 20 newsletters about health and education and employs some 45 persons.

A number of magazine publishers recently have entered the newsletter business. *Newsweek* last year started publishing *New Products & Processes Newsletter,* a spinoff of a column in the magazine's international section. McGraw-Hill, the New York publishing firm which puts out *Business Week,* publishes 19 newsletters — 12 of which have been started in the last five years. The acknowledged leader in the field is the Bureau of National Affairs, an independent research organization located in Washington. Its 650-member staff produces 42 publications. BNA president John Stewart told the *Washington Journalism Review* last year that his company takes in over $50 million a year.[7]

Findings of the Paperwork Commission

Since the information industry draws much of the data it uses from government sources, private research firms are acutely aware of the red tape that often makes it difficult to gain access to needed federal records. This is a frustration many citizens also know first-hand. "On the surface, red tape resembles other noxious byproducts we generate in the course of making things and rendering services we are eager to have," wrote Herbert Kaufman of the Brookings Institution. "More of what we want means more of what we don't want as well."[8]

The Federal Commission on Paperwork was established in 1976 by President Ford to study ways to eliminate bureaucratic barriers in the government's information network. In its final

[7] *Washington Journalism Review,* October 1977, p. 56.

[8] Herbert Kaufman, *Red Tape: Its Origins, Uses and Abuses* (1977), p. 60.

report, issued in January 1978, the commission recommended a "less is more" approach to the deluge of government reports and documents. The major thrust of the commission's findings was that Washington policymakers should take into account all costs of paperwork — including citizen frustration and administrative inefficiencies — as well as the substantial dollar cost. Private and public sectors spend more than $100 billion a year on paperwork, or about $500 per citizen, the commission estimated.

The commission recommended that federal forms be consolidated and that each agency use existing data whenever possible — including that collected by other agencies — instead of making redundant surveys and/or issuing repetitive forms. Other key recommendations included:

1. Creation of a new Cabinet-level Department of Administration to coordinate the flow of federal information between agencies and to facilitate public access to government data.

2. Creation of a government-wide information locating system that would enable an agency to determine if the data it needed was already on file or in the process of being collected.

3. Shortening regulations and writing them in easily understood language.

4. Making certain changes in the Freedom of Information Act[9] to foster data-sharing among government agencies while establishing more precise statutory definitions of confidentiality.

The commission's recommendations received mixed reviews. The suggestion that a Department of Administration could solve the "information glut" drew particular criticism. "We can encourage each department to tighten up its operations without hiring thousands of more bureaucrats to add to the paperwork," said Rep. Peter H. Kostmayer, D-Pa.[10]

One idea that met with general approval was the proposal to eliminate inconsistent and often conflicting federal information laws and practices. In its final recommendations, the Paperwork Commission urged adoption of government-wide criteria for ranking information according to its sensitivity. The most sensitive data would be kept confidential, but only in the face of compelling national interests or to preserve privacy rights. Less sensitive information would be permitted to circulate among agencies, while the least sensitive data would be made available to the public.

In August, Reps. Frank Horton, R-N.Y., Jack Brooks, D-

---

[9]Passed by Congress in 1966 and amended several times since, the Freedom of Information Act was designed to facilitate public access to government data that previously had been kept secret.

[10] Testimony before the House Government Operations Subcommittee on Government Information and Individual Rights, Oct. 18, 1977.

Texas, and Tom Steed, D-Okla., introduced a bill — the Paperwork and Red Tape Reduction Act of 1978 — which provided for establishment of an Office of Federal Information Management Policy in the Office of Management and Budget to oversee all facets of information activities in the federal government. The office would have wide responsibility for setting policy pertaining to federal information management activities. The bill also provided for the creation of a federal information locator office in the General Services Administration. Hearings on the bill are expected to be held sometime after the 96th Congress convenes next January.

Advances in Data Gathering

SINCE THE EARLIEST days of recorded history, when scribes preserved ancient lore on clay tablets, societies have stored information for future use. Temples originally were employed for this purpose. In Egypt, nearly every religious shrine housed a repository for holy documents. Historians credit the writings of Aristotle, the Greek philosopher, with encouraging Egyptian kings to amass collections of religious and secular information. The library at Alexandria, founded by the ruler Ptolemy, was the focal point of scholarship in the Hellenistic world. Before it was destroyed in 391 A.D., it contained over 700,000 scrolls.

From its origins to the present, the library has been considered a central source of information. Prior to the first century B.C., however, only priests and scholars could make use of the material contained in temple and royal libraries. The first public library, proposed by Gaius Julius Caesar, was opened in Rome sometime between 39 and 27 B.C. Roman emperors also maintained private collections of state documents and papers.

Following the collapse of the Roman Empire, Christians gathered in their churches and monasteries what writings they could salvage. With the founding of the abbey at Monte Casino in 529, the Benedictine Order began an intellectual tradition which carried ancient learning from Italy to institutions throughout Europe. From monastic beginnings, collections of manuscripts grew in Spain, France, Germany and England, often under the patronage of noble families. Bibles, interpretations of scriptures, codes of civil law, religious canons and the writings of church fathers comprised the core of what was considered useful information through the 12th century. Generally, this material was provided by monks and other clerks who spent their lives copying tomes of antiquity.

The invention of the printing press in 1437, at the height of the Renaissance, revolutionized the way people communicated with one another. Works of literature and scholarship no longer had to be painstakingly copied by hand, but could be reproduced in great quantities. Ideas that once were available only to a few could be shared with many. Printed books were more portable than manuscripts, and more easily handled and shelved. Bound and printed documents also could be catalogued and indexed in a manner that facilitated the retrieval of information. Along with the new accessibility of information came an increased secularization of knowledge, a trend that encouraged the growth of universities.

Development of Public Library System

As learning spread from Europe to the New World, techniques for collecting and disseminating information were further refined. In colonial America, where only the rich could afford book collections, the middle class turned to group buying, a device pioneered by Benjamin Franklin. He and his friends founded the Library Company of Philadelphia in 1731. Between 1750 and 1850, subscription libraries were formed in hundreds of towns, and the motivation for the public library system came from these groups. Franklin wrote in his *Autobiography:* "[Subscription] libraries have improved the general conversation of Americans, made the common tradesmen and farmers as intelligent as most gentlemen from other countries, and perhaps have contributed...to the stand so generally made throughout the colonies in defense of their privileges."[11]

The first public library of consequence opened in Boston in 1854. Mayor Josiah Quincy gave $5,000 for its founding, and the city petitioned the state for authority to levy a tax for library support. Early backers of public libraries emphasized the mission of the library to educate the public. Melvil Dewey, one of the founders of the American Library Association, wrote in the first issue of the *Library Journal* in 1876: "The school teaches [people] to read; the library must supply them with [information] which will serve to educate."

Today the United States possesses a wealth of public and research libraries. The Library of Congress, one of the world's great repositories of learning, occupies a unique position in America's information resource system. It is, in fact if not in name, the nation's central library. It provides services not only to Congress, but also to other libraries and information outlets throughout the country. Last year, the Library of Congress sup-

---

[11] Benjamin Franklin, *The Autobiography* (Modern Library Ed., 1950), p. 88.

plied nearly a half-million items to other institutions worldwide through inter-library loans.

Pressured by a growing demand for information, libraries have turned increasingly to automation as an answer to many of their problems.[12] The National Library of Medicine near Washington, D.C., is considered by many experts to be the model automated research library. Hospitals around the country have relied on its computer-run medical data service for over a decade.

" 'Everyone is entitled to know everything.' But this is a false slogan, characteristic of a false era; people also have the right not to know — the right not to have their divine souls stuffed with gossip, nonsense and vain talk. A person who works and leads a meaningful life does not need this excessive burdening flow of information."

Alexander Solzhenitsyn, address delivered at Harvard University, June 8, 1978.

Complete automation will be both unnecessary and too costly for most public libraries in the foreseeable future. But many already have modified and adapted some elements of automation to suit their own particular needs. "The rapidly expanding library," Paul Wasserman wrote in 1965, "faces the same type of problem as that which banks and insurance companies faced earlier — a burgeoning record-keeping system generated out of a volume of traffic and client service."[13]

The use of microfilm and other microforms is not a new development in library science. But in recent years libraries have stepped up their efforts to put their holdings on film. Libraries today are faced not only with a shortage of storage space and a burgeoning amount of new material, but also with serious deterioration of many books and documents. In addition to solving these problems, microfilm and other photo-reduction processes can give researchers easy access to the contents of rare books and manuscripts which otherwise would be impossible to study.

[12] See "Library Expansion," *E.R.R.*, 1967 Vol. I, pp. 410-418.
[13] Paul Wasserman, *The Librarian and the Machine* (1965), p. 26.

Man has devised machines to lighten his physical and mental labors from the earliest days of civilization. The abacus, a rudimentary counting instrument developed in ancient China, was a forerunner of both the first adding machine and the modern-day computer. Two philosopher-mathematicians, Blaise Pascal (1623-62), a Frenchman, and Gottfried Leibnitz (1646-1716), a German, are credited with designing the original mechanical calculators. In 1642, Pascal invented a gear-driven machine capable of adding and subtracting. Thirty years later, Leibnitz exhibited before the Academy of Paris a devise that could multiply, divide and extract square roots as well as add and subtract.

Invention of Problem-Solving Machines

Charles Babbage, a mathematics professor at Cambridge University, is regarded as the father of modern data processing. Using principles laid down by Pascal and Leibnitz, Babbage undertook in 1823 to construct a "difference machine" that would calculate and print such things as logarithm tables. The machine was almost completed when he abandoned it to develop an "analytical engine" that would automatically evaluate any mathematical formula. However, Babbage died in 1871 before it could be perfected.

The next important step in the evolution of computers came in connection with the 1890 United States census. The 1880 census, which enumerated 50 million persons, had taken seven years to complete. As a result, there was concern that the 1890 count would not be available before the end of the decade. Such a delay would have prevented reapportionment of seats in the House of Representatives as required by the Constitution. It was to avert a crisis of this kind that the U.S. Census Bureau made use of an invention by Herman Hollerith, a statistician from Buffalo, N.Y. In 1899, Hollerith had constructed an automatic data-handling machine that employed perforated cards. Thanks largely to this device, the census taken in 1890 was compiled in little more than two years.

Research initiated during World War II led to the development of ENIAC (Electric Numerical Integrator and Calculator), the first electronic computer. Two and one-half years in the making, ENIAC was introduced at the University of Pennsylvania in 1946. It solved its first problem, a question involving atomic physics, in two weeks. The machine contained 18,000 vacuum tubes and could carry out 5,000 additions a second. Today's information-storing computers contain transistors or microcircuits instead of tubes and can make as many as several billion calculations a second.

151

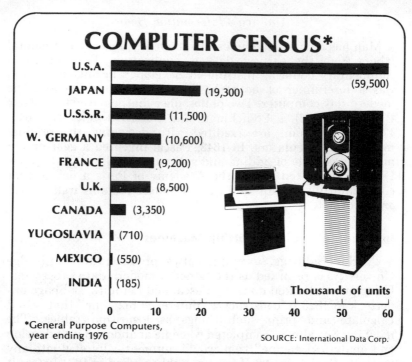

COMPUTER CENSUS*

	Thousands of units
U.S.A.	(59,500)
JAPAN	(19,300)
U.S.S.R.	(11,500)
W. GERMANY	(10,600)
FRANCE	(9,200)
U.K.	(8,500)
CANADA	(3,350)
YUGOSLAVIA	(710)
MEXICO	(550)
INDIA	(185)

*General Purpose Computers, year ending 1976

SOURCE: International Data Corp.

Confronted with a growing need for information in all fields, scientists have designed modern computers with memory systems capable of handling every imaginable kind of data. Whereas ancient scholars and librarians once served as custodians of the world's accumulated knowledge, computer information specialists now are assuming that role. The computer itself has proved most valuable as a kind of super-clerk, carrying out repetitive operations millions or trillions of times without ever becoming bored or tired and therefore error-prone.

Benefits and Risks in Computer Usage

The fact that computers are able to perform tasks in a fraction of the time required by human beings has transformed the field of information collection and retrieval. The machines are invaluable in keeping track of company payrolls, banking transactions and inventories; in helping law enforcement agencies handle criminal records; and speeding up the accounting procedures of America's credit card economy.

Computers also have found wide application in publishing. "The [uses] that are most suitable to the versatility of electronic technology are in the manipulation and rearrangement of lists, such as indexes, directories, parts of catalogues, compendia — any listing in which [information] used for one purpose can be reused for another."[14] The many computer-produced

[14] "Using the Computer for the Appropriate Job," *Publishers Weekly*, Dec. 4, 1967, p. 64.

publications in existence today include the whole array of catalogues and indexes issued by the Government Printing Office as well as a wide assortment of newspapers and magazines.

Both military and industrial planners use computers to simulate complex processes that would be too costly or dangerous to test in actual situations. At the Pentagon, nuclear war games are played by machine; at aerospace companies and auto factories design problems are worked out by computer before the first prototype is built. In many industries, computers are considered more reliable than workers, a fact that has led to increased labor-management disputes over automation.[15]

Some degree of disenchantment with computers was inevitable. The trouble is that the computer, lacking judgment or compassion, is unable to distinguish between facts and information that may be half-true or totally erroneous. This presents a special problem in the area of consumer credit. Consumer advocate Ralph Nader is among those who maintain that credit bureau files often contain inaccurate or incomplete information. "The introduction of computers," Nader wrote, "can create its own set of problems. Although mechanical errors in the handling of information by people may be reduced, the probability of machine error is increased."[16] The Fair Credit Reporting Act of 1971 was designed to cope with the type of problem Nader cited, giving consumers the right to sue to gain access to credit data, and to petition for damages if it is proven inaccurate.

Future of Communications

A NEW APPLIANCE, the "home computer," is expected to come into widespread use by the middle of the 1980s. Several models already are available to the public. They are about the size of a suitcase and work with their own display screen or can be programmed to operate in conjunction with a television set. Home computers now on the market perform at the domestic level many tasks that larger computers perform for business and industry, acting as information terminals and calculators.

Industry analysts differ in their assessment of the public's

[15] Computerized photocomposition machines are capable of producing about 1,000 newspaper lines a minute. That is about 200 times the rate of production of a Linotype operator. The 1978 New York City newspaper strike resulted when local papers, citing automation as the reason, threatened to cut their pressroom crews by 70 percent.

[16] Ralph Nader, "The Dossier Invades the Home," *Saturday Review*, April 17, 1971, p. 19.

willingness to learn how to use computers to organize household finances. If accepted by the public, home computers could alter the pattern of daily life. In the foreseeable future, engineers, scientists, clerks, bookkeepers and many salesmen could work almost entirely at home, using computer terminals and teleprinters to conduct their businesses. Occupations that supply ideas and information could become decentralized and thereby relieve some of the pressures of urbanization.

In combination with television, the personal computer of the future could transform any living room into a complete entertainment and resource center. In England, the government currently is conducting limited home experiments with telephone-television-computer hookups. The British model home computer, "Videodata," has a limited program capacity, bringing users information on such items as airline schedules, restaurant prices and stock quotations. But it suggests how similar machines with expanded program potential might serve as home libraries, giving households access to huge research data banks controlled by a central computer.

In less than a decade, personal computers have turned into a $3 billion industry and the end to growth is nowhere in sight. *The Wall Street Journal* reported earlier this year that as many as 100,000 Americans owned personal data processing units.[17] The trend has spawned thousands of specialty stores and a half-dozen magazines. One large firm in the home computer market is the Tandy Corp., which runs a chain of 6,000 electronics supply stores nationwide. The chain began selling so-called "mini-computers" last year for around $500 — about the same price as a good color television set. But most of the commercially available models come in kit form and require some knowledge of electronics to assembly and a certain amount of competence in programming to operate.

Home computers, like larger data processing units, run on electric current. It is conceivable that if the machines were widely used, they could place excessive demands on the nation's limited supply of electric power. The computer industry, riding the crest of the information boom, does not seem to regard that as a serious problem.

Disseminating Information on Cable TV

Cable television has the potential to make every television set a veritable encyclopedia of information. Cable TV systems capable of delivering up to 144 channels to each subscriber now operate in a number of markets, with channels used for entertainment programming, weather and stock market reports

---

[17] See *The Wall Street Journal*, Feb. 4, 1978.

Home Video Recorders

Prime time, "the family hour" and the late, late show soon may become misnomers. Home videotape machines, which record and play back programs, have liberated TV viewers from what *Newsweek* magazine called "the tyranny of television schedules." First put on the market two years ago for upward of $3,000, videotape recorders (VTRs) now retail for around $800. As the price declines further, industry spokesmen predict the machines will become as common in homes as stereo systems.

The VTR has obvious appeal. It can be attached to any TV set and automatically tape any program the viewer designates. It also can record one program while the set is tuned to another. Shows can be stored and played back or tapes can be erased and used again. There is, however, a chance that the machines, which are produced by nearly every major television manufacturer, could be declared illegal. Walt Disney Productions and Universal Studios are suing one company, Sony, charging that its model, the Betamax, violates federal copyright law by recording motion pictures shown on television.

and adult education courses. If cable television had a two-way, broad-band communications capability, channels could serve as instantaneous links to food stores, physicians' offices, banks and the like, displaying prices and other information that would allow people to tend to many of their needs without leaving home.

In the years to come, cable television could be an important medium for disseminating information on the community level. But nurturing community use of cable TV, which transmits video signals by wire rather than over the airwaves, has not been easy. According to David Hoke of the National Federation of

Computer Checkout

The grocery store checkout line — as standard a piece of Americana as one could expect to find — recently has taken on the aspect of science fiction. An increasing number of supermarkets around the country are replacing their old-fashioned cash registers with computer units capable of doing everything from taking stock inventory to thanking shoppers for their patronage.

The systems were introduced in stores several years ago as a means of speeding up checkout time and eliminating human error. Today, use has expanded to the point where computers promise to revolutionize the grocery business. Having shared few of the modern advances of other industries, food stores could benefit as computers decrease labor costs and help boost falling profits.

Many consumer groups, however, are not overly enthusiastic about the arrival of computers in the marketplace. Ellen Haas, director of the Community Nutrition Institute in Washington, D.C., expressed concern that the high cost of the systems would be passed on to the shopping public. "The industry is saying that computers will save them money, but there's no guarantee that it will be passed on to the consumer," she said. Others have expressed concern about the potential for price manipulation. But according to industry spokesmen, computer checkout systems virtually have abolished the problem of overcharging — one of the principal sources of consumer complaints.

Local Cable Programmers, "most communities are not aware that public access exists." A National Cable Television Association survey in 1976 reported that only 52 percent of the operators responding had broadcast community information programs.

The Supreme Court agreed in October to decide whether the Federal Communications Commission (FCC) can require cable television systems with at least 3,500 subscribers to designate one channel for use by the public, educational authorities and local governments. The 8th U.S. Circuit Court of Appeals ruled in 1976 that in ordering access to cable TV systems, the FCC had overstepped its authority.[18] Among those siding with the commission in the case is the American Civil Liberties Union, which maintains that the expansion of information "outlets for community self-expression...remains an objective of critical public importance."

"By 1985 the degree of automation of information will approach a hundred times that of today."

George Anderla, *Information in 1985* (1973)

There are some 3,700 cable television systems currently operating in the United States, serving 12.9 million homes. The industry estimates that the number of subscribers will grow to 20 million by 1980. Under FCC regulations, local governments are responsible for awarding cable franchise privileges, while cable operators themselves have the obligation of alloting time to community groups. But cable TV companies have been reluctant to give the communities they serve access to their broadcast facilities.

Long-Term Impact of New Technologies

Recent advances in communications technology have provided the means for developing highly efficient information systems. Video tape recorders and video discs, low-cost satellite receiving stations and expanding cable television networks not only promise to improve the distribution of data but also could transform the world as profoundly as the industrial revolution.

Considering the technological achievements of his day, 19th

---

[18] *Federal Communications Commission v. Midwest Video Corp.*

century British biologist Thomas H. Huxley wondered how men ultimately would use all of the work-saving machines they had invented. There will come a time, Huxley theorized, when mankind will possess "the means of obtaining extensive practical knowledge...on every earthly matter." Yet scientific and industrial progress, he believed, would not work to the advantage of future generations unless it was governed by moral principles that lie outside the realm of technology.[19] The present age still is wrestling with the implications of technological progress and with the systems it has evolved for organizing a hitherto unimaginable complexity of information.

"The introduction of computers can create its own set of problems. Although mechanical errors in the handling of information by people may be reduced, the probability of machine errors is increased."

Ralph Nader, 1971

Many of the great national debates during the last decade have been over issues involving information — the Pentagon Papers, Watergate and secret intelligence gathering. In the realm of politics as elsewhere, the old forms of power, such as money or material rewards, have become relatively insignificant. The new "power currency" is information, wrote John McHale.[20] And as societies come to depend more and more on computers, McHale predicted, "wealth [will be] generated with decreasing inputs of human energy, intervention and decision making."[21]

Some theorists foresee the eventual creation of information utilities that will function as electric and power companies do today. It is conceivable that such utilities could offer services to general business subscribers by the mid-1980s and to private individuals before the turn of the century.

A "new symbiosis," McHale wrote, will develop between man and the information-supplying machines he uses. As industrial societies progress along their present course, "automated systems will begin to assume the routine operations of their basic...functions, in much the same way that the autonomic ner-

---

[19] Thomas H. Huxley, "Science and Culture," *The Norton Anthology of English Literature,* Vol. II (1974), p. 1620.
[20] John McHale, *The Changing Information Environment* (1976), p. 1.
[21] *Ibid.,* p. 11.

International Communications

The decisions made at next year's meeting of the World Administrative Radio Conference (WRAC) in Geneva could shape the direction of international communications for decades to come. The purpose of the conference, held under the auspices of the United Nations, will be to allocate use of the entire electronic "spectrum." The spectrum is a limited resource that includes waves and frequencies for carrying radio signals, television pictures and telephone messages. How it is divided will have a direct bearing on the economic and political status of all nations.

The industrialized powers of the West, particularly the United States, have had a longstanding monopoly on the spectrum. But the developing countries that now are demanding to be full participants in the world economic system also are demanding a greater share of the electronic spectrum — whether or not they now possess the capabilities to use it. Should Third World governments, in their determination to have more international and internal broadcast space, vote as a bloc, they could get what they want. At the very least, it seems certain that Western nations will be forced into the position of having to bargain for communication privileges they once took for granted.

vous system regulates the...human organism." The demands for more effective information management have occasioned warnings that a blind commitment to progress should be tempered by extreme caution. How these conflicting ideas are reconciled could determine whether man will benefit from his reliance on data systems or will become a slave to the technology he has designed to do his bidding.

▼▼▼

Selected Bibliography

Books

Adams, Henry, *The Education of Henry Adams,* Modern Library, 1976.
Adams, J. Mack and Douglas H. Haden, *Social Effects of Computer Use and Misuse,* Wiley, 1976.
Anuta, Larry D., *Information Game,* Surevelation Press, 1976.
Davisson, William I., *Information Processing,* Plenum Press, 1970.
Hammer, Donald P., ed., *Information Age: Its Development, Its Impact,* Scarecrow Press, 1976.
McHale, John, *The Changing Information Environment,* Westview Press, 1976.
Pynchon, Thomas, *V.,* Lippincott, 1963.
Rothman, Milton, *Cybernetic Revolution: Thought and Control in Man and Machine,* International Library, 1972.

Articles

"Coming: Another Revolution in the Use of Computers," *U.S. News & World Report,* July 19, 1976.
Computerworld, selected issues.
"Information: The Ultimate Resource," *The Futurist,* February 1978.
Irwin, Manley R. and Steven C. Johnson, "The Information Economy and Public Policy," *Science,* March 18, 1977.
Kolata, Gina B., "Information Theory: A Surprising Proof," *Science,* Jan. 6, 1978.
Madnick, Stuart E., "Trends in Computers and Computering: The Information Utility," *Science,* March 18, 1977.
Selige, Susan, "Newsletters: The Fourth and a Half Estate," *Washington Journalism Review,* October 1977.
Walsh, John, "Carter Reorganization Panel Says Federal Data Processing Is Lagging," *Science,* Sept. 15, 1978.

Reports and Studies

Editorial Research Reports, "Approach to Thinking Machines," 1962 Vol. II, p. 537; "Reappraisal of Computers," 1971 Vol. I, p. 347; "Computer Crime," 1978 Vol. I, p. 1.
General Accounting Office, "Ways to Improve Management of Federally Funded Computerized Models," Aug. 23, 1976.
"The U.S. Economy 1990," The Conference Board, 1972.

MEDIA REFORMERS

by

William V. Thomas

**Dec. 23
1977**

(**Report update:** A new development since the original publication of this report was the Federal Trade Commission's vote on Feb. 22, 1978, to consider restrictions on television advertising aimed at children. The commission stopped short of proosing an outright ban on certain commercials as recommended by an FTC staff report. The proposal under consideration would prohibit any type of TV commercial directed at audiences containing "a significant proportion" of children "too young to understand" the purpose of the ad. The proposed rule would also prohibit commercials for sugared products seen by older children. Such ads, according to the media reform group Action for Children's Television (ACT), post serious health risks to youngsters.)

MEDIA REFORMERS

L IKE MANY AMERICAN institutions in the last decade, the press and broadcast media have come under increasing criticism. The old debate over their rights and responsibilities has been marked recently by the appearance of hundreds of citizen-organized reform groups. Representing a broad cross-section of political and religious leanings, they are drawn together by the common goal of gaining a greater voice in setting media standards. As the number of so-called "watchdog" organizations has grown, so, it seems, has their determination. Network executives and newspaper editors "may not know it yet," said a spokesman for a religious group, "but they're about to be hit by a revolution."[1]

The charge most frequently made by reform groups is that the press and commercial television networks are more concerned with profits than principles of accuracy and fairness. Particular complaints cover a wide range of alleged faults from biased news coverage in daily papers to a distorted depiction of life on television. Yet underlying nearly every aspect of the current protest is a belief that the First Amendment's guarantee of freedom of the press also implies the right of readers and viewers to help in determining how that freedom should be used.[2]

A general dissatisfaction with news ethics, prompted partly by Nixon administration attacks on the press,[3] has been credited with encouraging the appearance of journalistic self-criticism in many of the nation's papers as well as an increase in space allotted to letters to the editor. Under viewer pressure, a few television advertisers have even said they would withdraw their support from shows that depict violence. But, according to Charles B. Seib, ombudsman for *The Washington Post,* media owners "have not faced up to...the fundamental issues" being raised by angry consumers.[4]

Reed Irvine, chairman of Accuracy in Media (AIM), an organization that monitors press and television news reporting, takes the position that the big media corporations have used

---

[1] Carl Richardson of the Church of God, quoted in *TV Guide,* Oct. 1, 1977. The Church of God, which claims 457,000 members, organized a TV boycott the week of April 10-16, 1977, to protest "televised violence and sex."
[2] See "Access to the Media," *E.R.R.,* 1974 Vol. I, pp. 447-470.
[3] See "First Amendment and Mass Media," *E.R.R.,* 1970 Vol. I, pp. 41-60.
[4] Charles B. Seib, *The Washington Post,* Nov. 5, 1976.

their power in a biased and therefore potentially dangerous fashion. AIM calls itself a watchdog group devoted to promoting "fairness in reporting on critical issues," which it feels are often shaded by the media's liberal perspective. Others, however, have accused AIM of allowing a politically conservative bias of its own to color much of its activity. Speaking last year to a meeting of journalists, Irvine expressed AIM's basic philosophy this way: "No society is truly free without a free press, but the existence of a free press does not necessarily guarantee a free society. Unfortunately, history indicates that a free press may contribute to its own destruction and to the destruction of all other freedoms.... There is some reason to question whether or not we have gone too far for our own good, perhaps creating a monster which may [destroy] many of the freedoms we cherish, including freedom of the press."[5]

While many reform groups agree on the general goal of increasing access to the media, most of them seek to further their own particular interests. Some have been mobilized to challenge a single news story or broadcast, as was the case when various pro-gun groups joined together in 1975 to protest a CBS-TV program, "The Guns of Autumn," that was critical of hunting. Among business corporations, General Motors and the Mobil Oil Co., monitor the media and run aggressive "opinion advertising" to correct what they consider erroneous news coverage of matters relating to their operations.

Campaign Against Violence on Television

The one issue that seems to unite the often disparate factions of the media reform movement is television violence, which, it is claimed, gives young watchers a warped conception of human behavior. That theory received considerable national attention in October when 15-year-old Ronald Zamora of Miami was tried and convicted of murdering an elderly woman. The defense attorney contended that Zamora was innocent of willful homicide because "he was suffering from and acted under the influence of prolonged, intense, involuntary, subliminal television intoxication.... The tube became [the boy's] parents, his school and church." Zamora, he added, had been so conditioned to kill by watching "endless hours" of televised violence that murder itself was no more than the "acting out of a television script."

A Dade County (Fla.) jury found Zamora guilty and sentenced him to 25 years to life in prison. But the trial, which incidentally was televised in Florida as part of a special experiment allowing cameras in court, raised a number of questions about the effects of watching dramatized mayhem on television. A University of Pennsylvania study in 1976 revealed

---

[5] Speech to the Missouri Press Convention in St. Louis, Oct. 22, 1976.

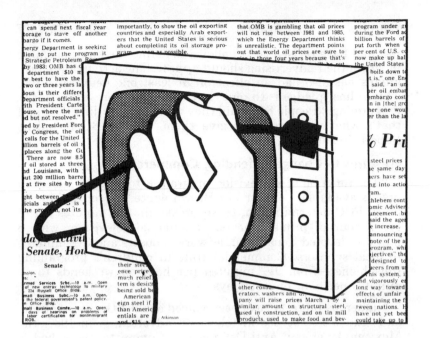

that the index of television violence that year had increased sharply over the previous year—despite a network policy of setting aside a two-hour "family viewing" period free of violence each weekday evening. The most violent shows, the survey found, were those broadcast on Saturday morning and aimed exclusively at children. The study concluded "that while all viewers absorb TV 'lessons' of fear, suspicion and mistrust, children are the most affected by the 'mean world syndrome' of television programing."[6]

Figures cited in July by the National Parent-Teachers Association, which last year began a vigorous campaign against violence on television, indicated that the average child now watches 6 to 6½ hours of television a day, while preschool children view 25 hours of television a week. "We don't think [children] can watch...rape and murder night after night, week after week without being affected by it," said William M. Young, project director of the PTA's current boycott of products that sponsor violent shows. Although some critics of television violence believe that protests should be directed at the networks instead of program sponsors, reform groups have been successful in forcing changes in some programs through the threat of product boycotts.

Media Watch, a monthly newsletter published by the National Citizens Committee for Broadcasting, a Washington-based reform organization, reported in February that a number of companies are concerned about demonstrations of buyer un-

---

[6] *Violence Profile, No. 8,* 1976.

Editorial Research Reports   *Dec. 23, 1977*

rest and have revised their policies to define the kinds of shows in which their advertising should appear. The activity of reform groups has also had an effect on at least one network, NBC, which has pledged to cut back its support for violent programing. "People have said they want another direction, and that's what we're going to give them," said NBC President Robert T. Howard.[7]

Pressures to Change Offending Commercials

"The function of a television program is to make commercial breaks available," author Les Brown wrote.[8] According to the latest FCC determination, those breaks fill 9½ minutes out of every hour of prime time on commercial television, with 6 minutes devoted to national network sponsors and 3½ minutes to local sponsors. Commercial time in children's programing runs higher—from 9½ minutes per hour on weekends to 12 minutes per hour on weekdays.[9]

Numerous protests have been voiced against the use of ethnic and sexual stereotypes in television advertising. In 1967, the Mexican-American Anti-Defamation Committee launched a campaign against the "Frito Bandito," a Mexican cartoon character used in television ads for Frito-Lay corn chips. After four years of controversy, during which time protest groups picketed supermarkets and TV stations in the Southwest, the Frito-Lay Co. finally agreed to discontinue "Frito Bandito" commercials.

The National Organization for Women, whose media task force monitors television commercials, has managed to have some ads "offensive to women" changed or canceled. But a recent NOW survey of 1,241 TV commercials concluded that most product advertisers continue to portray women in a bad light, "as dependent, unintelligent, submissive creatures who are the adjuncts of men."[10]

A U.S. Civil Rights Commission study on women in the media reported that women are misrepresented not only in television advertising but also in most network comedy shows where they frequently are seen in demeaning roles. "The women in situation comedies still tend to be subordinate to the men in their lives," the study said. "Mary [in the "Mary Tyler Moore Show"] calls her boss 'Mr. Grant' even though everyone else calls him 'Lou.' Edith [in "All in the Family"] scoots into the kitchen to fetch Archie a beer and rarely fails to have dinner on

---

[7] Quoted in *Media Watch,* January-February 1977.
[8] Les Brown, *Television: The Business Behind the Box* (1971), p. 65.
[9] Federal Communications Commission, "Report and Policy Statement on Children's Television Programs," *Federal Register,* 1974, p. 39400.
[10] NOW survey cited in the U.S. Civil Rights Commission study "Window Dressing on the Set," August 1977, p. 12.

Rating Television Violence

The following rankings were compiled by the National Citizens Committee for Broadcasting over a two-week period during the spring 1977 television season. They were based on the number and length of violent incidents per show compared to the total time and incidents of violence in all prime time programing. NCCB defines violence as "an overt expression of physical force (with or without weapon) against oneself or other.... An action to be considered violent must be plausible and credible and must include human or human-like characters. It may be an intentional or accidental action, humorous or serious or a combination of both...."

10 Least Violent Shows		10 Most Violent Shows	
Program	**Network**	**Program**	**Network**
Alice	CBS	Starsky and Hutch	ABC
All in the Family	CBS	Wonder Woman	ABC
Bob Newhart	CBS	Baa Baa Black Sheep	NBC
Phyllis	CBS	Baretta	ABC
Maude	CBS	Walt Disney	NBC
Good Times	CBS	Rockford Files	NBC
Welcome Back Kotter	ABC	Quincy	NBC
Fish	ABC	Charlie's Angels	ABC
Happy Days	ABC	Police Woman	NBC
M.A.S.H.	CBS	Kojak	CBS

the table by 6 p.m."[11] The commission's appraisal of television programing itself became a target of criticism in the press. Its recommendations for policing the networks were greeted as an exercise in bureaucratic overkill.

The current focus of the campaign to reform television commercials is on advertising directed toward children. Action for Children's Television (ACT), a public-interest group with the goal of improving children's programing, asked the FCC in 1970 to eliminate all advertising from children's shows and to require every television station to broadcast at least 14 hours of commercial-free children's programs a week. In response to the ACT petition and other expressions of citizen concern, the FCC in 1974 created a special unit to study problems related to children's television. Since that time, the commission's policy has been to rely on the sponsors and producers of children's shows to adopt their own standards of self-regulation, governing commercials and program content. Advertising revenue pays for the programs, the FCC reasoned, and banning all ads on children's television "could have a very damaging effect on the amount and quality of the shows."[12]

[11] *Ibid.*, p. 23.
[12] "Report and Policy Statement on Children's Television Programs," *op. cit.*, p. 39399.

The commission's approach has not pleased the critics, who say it has tended to place the interests of broadcasters above the public interest. "In view of the FCC's reluctance to force producers to limit advertising," said Maureen Harmonay of ACT, "we have requested permission to air counter-commercials that inform parents and children about the hazards of certain foods and other products advertised on TV." In November, the U.S. Court of Appeals for the District of Columbia upheld an FCC rule exempting most product com-mercials from the obligations of the "fairness doctrine" *(see p. 171)*, which requires stations to broadcast opposing opinions. However, the appeals court ordered the commission to consider requiring stations to set aside one hour a week for the presenta-tion of messages and lengthier programing by members of local communities and public-interest spokesmen.

News Council's Forum for Grievances

Since its founding in 1973, the National News Council has proven to be one of the most respected news monitoring organizations in the country. Set up under the auspices of the Twentieth Century Fund, the independent council, composed of 18 voluntary members, has two main goals: "to examine and report on complaints concerning the accuracy and fairness of news reporting in the United States [and] to initiate studies and report on issues involving freedom of the press."

In judging the alleged misdeeds of the news media, however, it has no legal authority to enforce its decisions. Like the 24-year-old British Press Council, on which it is modeled, its power is derived solely from its ability to influence public opinion. Yet that power, wrote Executive Director William B. Arthur, "is totally dependent on the judgment of editors to publish the council's findings."[13]

Although some major news organizations, including *The New York Times* and the Associated Press, opposed its creation in fear that it would breed an atmosphere of regulation, the National News Council has received considerable praise from many leaders in journalism for its professional standards. But its work remains largely unknown to the public. In its 1975 report on ethics, the American Society of Newspaper Editors said the council's "integrity...is without question.... It has es-tablished a record that deserves more attention than either editors or the public have so far given it."

In January 1977, CBS became the first major broadcast network to pledge its cooperation with the council. CBS Chair-

[13] William B. Arthur, "The News Council Lives!" *The Bulletin of the American Society of Newspaper Editors*, November-December 1973, p. 6.

Major National Media Reform Groups

Accuracy in Media (AIM), Washington	Corrects alleged errors or omissions in news reporting
Action for Children's Television (ACT), Newtonville, Mass.	Works for improvement of children's television programing
Alternate Media Center, (AMC), New York	Studies the uses of cable television and ways in which citizens can gain access to the medium
Aspen Institute Program on Communication and Society, Washington	Studies communications policy issues and publishes books and research papers
Cable Television Information Center, Washington	Monitors legal developments affecting cable television and assists local governments in establishing cable TV operations
Citizens Communications Center, Washington	A nonprofit public interest law firm specializing in communications cases before FCC and courts
National Association for Better Broadcasting (NABB), Los Angeles	The first national consumer group to promote the public interest in broadcasting, it evaluates network programing and participates in hearings before Congress and FCC
National Black Media Coalition (NBMC), Washington	A coalition of over 70 black media reform groups promoting minority needs in national broadcasting
National Citizens Committee for Broadcasting (NCCB), Washington	Seeks to make broadcasting responsive to public interest
National Federation of Community Broadcasters (NFCB), Washington	Represents the interests of community radio stations before the FCC and other federal agencies
National News Council, New York	Examines complaints of inaccuracy and unethical conduct by news-gathering organizations
National Organization for Women, Media Task Force, Washington	Promotes the positive image of women in the media and monitors the FCC
Office of Communication of the United Church of Christ, New York	Provides assistance in negotiating public grievances with local broadcasting stations
Public Advertising Council, Los Angeles	Produces public service announcements for public interest groups
Reporters Committee for Freedom of the Press, Washington	Offers legal defense and research services for journalists

169

man William Paley said the council "has furnished an impartial and expert group to which aggrieved parties can appeal for review in the interest of fair treatment by the news media."[14] Paley added that CBS News will report any council findings adverse to the network. In a further effort to publicize the council's proceedings, the *Columbia Journalism Review*, a bimonthly media magazine, recently began carrying reports of its decisions.[15]

More than 450 complaints have been ruled on by the National News Council in its four years of existence. In November, for example, it decided that an NBC News documentary entitled "Danger! Radioactive Waste" was "seriously flawed" in reporting two instances of possible radioactive harm to persons and animals. The council said it could not find evidence for a portion of the program which suggested radioactive waste material caused medical problems for one family and some cattle.

NBC responded that it stands by the facts presented in the show, but promised it would carefully look into the complaints. Among allegations currently under investigation are: (1) charges by the Teamsters Union against *Time* magazine for its reporting last July of mismanagement of a union pension fund; and (2) a grievance filed against WBBM-TV, a CBS affiliate in Chicago, for its broadcast of a news series in March that allegedly gave the impression the drug Laetrile "was effective in combating cancer."

In an attempt to bridge the gap between the public and the press, a small number of regional news councils have been started in this country and Canada. According to the National News Council, there are at present five regional media review organizations in the United States: the Minnesota Newspaper Association, the Iowa Freedom of Information Council, the Delaware News Council, the Honolulu Community-Media Council, and the Riverside, Calif., Press Council. The Ontario Press Council, the only such group in Canada, was created in 1972 when eight Ontario dailies[16] agreed to establish a "self-governing council...to control and discipline the press and other news media."[17]

---

[14] Quoted in an Associated Press interview, Jan. 25, 1977.

[15] The *Columbia Journalism Review* began its coverage of National News Council activity in its March-April 1977 issue.

[16] The *Brantford Expositor, The Kitchener-Waterloo Record, The London Free Press, The Hamilton Spectator, The Ottawa Citizen, The Owen Sound Sun-Times, The Toronto Star* and *The Windsor Star.*

[17] From a 1968 report of the Royal Commission on civil rights in Ontario, quoted in *The Bulletin of the American Society of Newspaper Editors,* January 1974, p. 13.

Matters of Federal Regulation

TRADITIONALLY, the First Amendment rights to freedom of speech and of the press have been invoked by broadcasters and publishers to defend their operations from government interference. But increasingly, public-interest groups have begun to cite those same rights to justify their demands for access to the media. Pointing to the growing number of communications companies that control newspapers as well as radio and television outlets,[18] reformers contend that today's giant media monopolies pose a dangerous threat to individual freedom of expression.

"Freedom of the press must be something more than a guarantee of the property rights of media owners," wrote law professor Jerome A. Barron, a leading advocate of greater public access to mass communication.[19] Barron argued this theory before the Supreme Court in 1974 in a case in which an unsuccessful candidate for state office in Florida, Pat L. Tornillo, was denied the right to reply to a critical editorial in *The Miami Herald*. Arguing that the concentration of news media ownership was a potential abridgement of rights assured by the First Amendment, Barron maintained the establishment of a federal right-to-reply law was needed to offset the Supreme Court's 1964 decision in *New York Times v. Sullivan*. In the 1964 case, the Supreme Court ruled that in order to win a libel judgment, a public figure or other newsworthy person must prove he was the victim of a deliberate, false accusation published with "actual malice" in mind.

The court decided unanimously against Tornillo's right-to-reply petition, emphasizing that the First Amendment gave editors final authority over what should be published in their papers. However, since then the court has retreated somewhat from its 1964 position on libel. In at least two cases, the court has limited the broad protection of news organizations by drawing a narrow definition of "public figures."[20] In the 1974 case of *Gertz v. Robert Welsh*, the court ruled that Elmer Gertz, a civil-rights activist and author, was not a public figure. In a similar ruling in 1976, *Time* magazine had to pay damages for inaccurately reporting information about a prominent Florida socialite, Mary Alice Firestone, whom the court determined was not a "public figure" because she played no major role "in the affairs of society."

[18] See "News Media Ownership," *E.R.R.*, 1977 Vol. I, pp. 183-202.
[19] Jerome A. Barron, *Freedom of the Press for Whom?* (1973), p. iv.
[20] See "The Demise of the Public Figure Doctrine," by John J. Watkins, in *Journal of Communications,* summer 1977.

Unlike the press, broadcasting is already subject to right-to-reply laws. In 1959, the FCC set forth its "fairness doctrine," requiring radio and television stations to air opposing points of view on public issues. The doctrine was extended in 1967 to require broadcasters to notify persons or groups when they were the subject of criticism in on-the-air discussions of controversial issues and to give them an appropriate opportunity for rebuttal.

The Supreme Court upheld the constitutionality of the fairness doctrine in the 1969 *Red Lion Broadcasting* decision,[21] in which the court decided that a radio station that had broadcast a "personal attack" had to provide reply time free of charge. The court declared that the fairness doctrine was necessary "in view of the...scarcity of broadcast frequencies, the government's role in allocating those frequencies, and the legitimate claims of those unable without government assistance to gain access to those frequencies for the expression of their views...."

The need for federal regulation of broadcasting became evident shortly after the invention of radio. While the medium was still in its infancy, Congress passed the Radio Act of 1912, which gave the Department of Commerce the authority to distribute operating licenses. But by the early 1920s, there were so many stations on the air, some of them using the same frequencies, that listeners often had trouble receiving clear, consistent reception. With radio station owners clamoring for the enforcement of power and frequency assignments, Congress created the Federal Radio Commission in 1927, designating the public interest as the most important criterion by which it should regulate the radio industry.

The Federal Communications Commission, established by the Communications Act of 1934, replaced the FRC. Its jurisdiction was expanded to cover both wire and wireless interstate transmissions. Through its license renewal authority, the FCC was empowered to hold local broadcasters accountable for the way in which they used the public airwaves. The Supreme Court affirmed the FCC's charter in a 1940 ruling in which it decided that:

> ...[N]o person is to have anything in the nature of a property right as a result of the granting of a license. Licenses are limited to a maximum of three years' duration, may be revoked, and need not be renewed. Thus the channels presently occupied remain free for a new assignment to another licensee in the interest of the listening public. Plainly it is not the purpose of the FCC to protect the licensee against competition, but to protect the public.[22]

---

[21] *Red Lion Broadcasting v. Federal Communications Commission,* 395 U.S. 369.
[22] *Federal Communications Commission v. Sanders Brothers Radio Station,* 309 U.S. 470, 475.

The coming of television not only increased the number of broadcast stations nationwide but made it necessary for the FCC to adopt regulations suitable to the new medium. In an effort to bring television to as many communities as possible, the commission generally awarded large cities three VHF (very high frequency) channels. By 1945, it had assigned or reserved all available VHF channels, even though channels in some sparsely populated regions went unused for years. As the demand for television grew in the 1950s and 1960s, the FCC opened the UHF (ultra high frequency) range of channels (14 through 83) for use by both commercial and public broadcasting.

Through the years, the stated aim of FCC policy has been to promote local ownership of broadcast outlets. But in the so-called "prime market" cities—cities with the biggest potential audiences—"absentee" media corporations, including the networks, control many of the radio and television stations. Critics of the FCC contend that it has never actively enforced its local ownership policy in a way that would discourage the networks from purchasing choice local stations.

FCC Action on Licensing and Programing

Newton N. Minow, upon being named FCC chairman by President Kennedy in 1961, quickly identified himself as an outspoken critic of commercial television, describing its fare as a "wasteland." He told the National Association of Broadcasters: "...[W]hen television is bad, nothing is worse. I invite you to sit down in front of your television set when [a] station goes on the air...and keep your eyes glued to that set until the station signs off. I can assure you that you will observe a vast wasteland. You will see a procession of game shows, audience participation shows, formula comedies about totally unbelievable families...violence, sadism, murder...private eyes, gangsters, more violence, and cartoons. And endless, commercials—many screaming, cajoling and offending...."[23]

Minow warned that the FCC would use its license renewal power to force broadcasters to upgrade their offerings. "Renewal will not be *pro forma* in the future," he said. "There is nothing permanent or sacred about a broadcast license." His warnings marked the beginning of a period of increased commission activity, particularly in educational or "public" television, which it encouraged as an alternative to commercial TV. The first important backing came in 1962 when Congress authorized the federal government to make grants for the construction of noncommercial television stations. An amendment to the Communications Act of 1952 prohibited the FCC from interfering with the actual purchase of a broadcast facility.

---

[23] Speech to the National Association of Broadcasters, Washington, D.C., May 9, 1961.

However, Minow, who was determined to increase the number of educational television channels, held up FCC approval of the sale of a New York station to a commercial group until non-commercial buyers could be found. His action, in 1962, drew heated criticism from network officials, who complained to the White House that the commission had overstepped its bounds. But President Kennedy gave Minow his full support. "You keep this up!" the President told him.[24]

Later, Minow virtually assured the future of public television when he persuaded Congress to pass a law requiring all television sets sold in the United States after January 1963 to be equipped with VHF as well as UHF channels. Previously, according to television historian Erik Barnouw, "set manufacturers, many of whom had VHF stations, had been in no hurry to spread the competition."[25]

There was no mistaking the government's anti-monopoly attitude toward the television networks in the Kennedy administration. In 1963, under Minow's leadership, the FCC banned the "option clause" in contracts between commercial networks and their local affiliates. The clauses gave the networks control over large blocs of time on affiliate stations. The elimination of the "option clause," however, had only a minimal effect on commercial programing, since most stations continued to fill their schedules with network shows.

Facilitating Access to the Media

THE FOUNDING FATHERS believed that the free flow of information and ideas was necessary to the function of democracy in America. But that ideal, some observers suggest, is being threatened by mergers and acquisitions in the communications industry. The concern is that the concentration of ownership reduces journalistic competition and, it is feared, the sense of responsibility to the public. As Congress prepares to rewrite the Federal Communications Act fully for the first time since 1934, these matters seem certain to receive legislative attention. The House Interstate and Foreign Commerce Subcommittee on Communications hopes to begin a draft revision of the act in January.

According to the author of a study on "cross-ownership," 60 million Americans live "in areas where at least one newspaper

[24] Quoted in Erik Barnouw, *Tube of Plenty: The Evolution of American Television* (1975), p. 303.
[25] *Ibid.*, p. 303.

Campaign Against Cigarette Advertising

The 1964 Surgeon General's report linking smoking and cancer marked the beginning of a vigorous campaign by anti-smoking groups to have cigarette commercials banned from radio and television. Under pressure from the American Cancer Society and other health and consumer organizations, the Federal Communications Commission ruled in 1967 that broadcasters were required under the fairness doctrine to make air time available for anti-smoking messages, since the pro-smoking messages contained in cigarette ads were judged a controversial matter of legitimate public interest.

As a result, the commission's order opened the way for thousands of messages warning of the dangers of smoking. By 1969, cigarette sales had dropped by more than 12 billion from the 540 billion cigarettes sold the previous year.

In 1970, Congress passed legislation that prohibited all cigarette commercials from radio and television. Subsequently, the FCC ruled broadcasters were no longer required to carry anti-smoking messages, and the spots all but disappeared. The following year, cigarette sales began to increase steadily, reaching a new peak of 620 billion in 1976.

Cigarette ads in newspapers and magazines were unaffected by the ban. They simply did not "generate the same kind of outrage that TV commercials engendered," former Sen. Frank E. Moss (D Utah, 1959-1976) said. However, the tobacco industry agreed in 1971 to disclose the tar and nicotin content of the cigarettes they advertised in print.

and one television station have the same owner."[26] While many owners maintain that joint newspaper-broadcast operations afford customers superior service, media reform groups across the country are almost unanimous in viewing them as a threat to public access and independent news coverage. In January, the Supreme Court is expected to hear arguments on the constitutionality of the cross-ownership question. Over 200 media combinations in 44 states could be affected by the outcome.

At issue in the case, *American Newspaper Publishers Association v. National Citizens Committee for Broadcasting,* is whether newspaper owners may be prohibited from acquiring radio and television stations in the same city in which their papers are published, and whether the FCC or the courts are empowered to order divestiture where newspaper and broadcast facilities are co-owned in a single "market" area. The Department of Justice has long contended that cross-ownership is an

---

[26] William T. Gormley Jr., "How Cross-Ownership Affects News-Gathering," *Columbia Journalism Review,* May-June 1977, p. 38. Gormley is the author of "The Effects of Newspaper-Television Cross-Ownership on News Homogeneity," a study published in 1975, funded by the John and Mary R. Markle Foundation.

antitrust violation in that it virtually eliminates competition for advertising revenue.

An FCC ruling in 1975 prohibited common control of newspapers and radio and television stations but allowed joint operations to continue in localities having only one daily newspaper and one broadcast outlet. However, the U.S. Court of Appeals for the District of Columbia ordered the commission to apply the rule to all media combinations so long as the public interest is not harmed.

The American Newspaper Publishers Association has contended that the appeals court went beyond its authority in the review of FCC decisions. The publishers association argued that in the licensing of broadcasters—many of whom also happened to own newspapers—the commission had declared they were serving the public interest. In a brief to the Supreme Court, ANPA said: "The prospective rules promulgated by the FCC and the retrospective divestiture required by the court of appeals seriously impair the constitutionally protected right to publish a newspaper.... Moreover, these rules will prevent broadcasters—often the only persons in a community who can combine journalistic expertise with adequate capital—from starting a new daily newspaper or acquiring an existing newspaper which otherwise might cease publication."

Should the appeals court ruling stand, cross-ownership in dozens of cities would be broken up. In early December, *The Washington Post* and *The Detroit News* announced plans to trade company-owned television stations in the two cities. The exchange, which will not become final until it gains FCC approval, is seen as a response to the divestiture decision by the court of appeals.

Udall's Bill to Aid Independent Newspapers

In a related effort aimed at helping independent newspapers survive, Rep. Morris K. Udall (D Ariz.) in October introduced a bill to create a trust fund to finance estate tax liabilities incurred by small weekly or daily papers. The fund would be supported by contributions from individual newspapers that stand to benefit from it and would be open only to papers not owned by a chain[27] or a public corporation. The American Newspaper Publishers Association reports that 1,762 daily newspapers were published in the United States in 1976 and, according to newspaper analyst John Morton, six of every ten were under group—chain—control.[28]

Media critic Ben H. Bagdikian, a professor of journalism at

---

[27] Udall's bill defines a chain as a company owning two or more newspapers.
[28] Morton is with the Washington office of the New York-based brokerage firm of Colin, Hochstin Co. He issues the *John Morton Newspaper Research* newsletter.

the University of California at Berkeley, said the bill "is a good idea for the remaining papers, mostly small, that are family held...and for people who start up a paper and build it up so it has a great deal of value.... It's medicine applied late, but better late than never."[29] The ANPA, which opposes divestiture, said it supports Udall's bill "as an important first step" in correcting present tax inequities that fall the hardest on small independent newspapers.

Many who favor the dismantling of the giant media corporations contend that diversity is not necessarily synonymous with size. Concentrations of ownership, they add, more often tend to foster a uniformity of judgment rather than a free traffic of varying opinion. Typical of this thought is a comment by Jim Hoge, editor-in-chief of the Chicago *Sun-Times* and *Daily News:* "All the good will in the world by conglomerates...is just not the same as a number of different voices owned by different groups."[30]

The current upsurge in media "empire building" began in the 1960s and is now marked by acquisitions as diverse as film production companies, book publishing enterprises and cable television systems. In contrast to those who look upon this development with misgivings, CBS President John D. Backe argues that only big communication corporations are strong enough to oppose the excesses of big government. "This is an age," he said recently, "when public opinion is the target of every special interest and special pleader. So it is very important that our journalistic and communications institutions be strong enough and diverse enough to resist those who want to foist their particular ideology on the public."[31]

Community Programing on Cable Television

Another "access" issue centers on cable television. The Federal Communications Commission ruled in 1976 that all U.S. cable television systems must provide community access to their facilities. But nurturing public use of cable TV, which transmits video signals by wire rather than over the airwaves, has not been easy. According to David Hoke of the National Federation of Local Cable Programers, "most communities are not aware that public access exists." A National Cable Television Association survey in 1976 reported that only 52 per cent of the operators responding had broadcast community-produced programs.

The idea of participatory television is relatively new. "Community people have long been oriented to the passive role of

---

[29] Quoted in *The Washington Post,* Oct. 7, 1977.
[30] Quoted in *U.S. News & World Report,* Aug. 15, 1977.
[31] Quoted in *The Washington Post,* Dec. 2, 1977.

broadcast television viewing," Hoke said. "Users do not generally break down the doors of access centers or operator-provided
production facilities just because they are available."[32] Communities need to be educated about cable television and the opportunities provided by access, he added.

At present, there are 3,700 cable television systems operating
in the United States, serving nearly 12 million households. The
industry estimates that the number of subscribers will grow to
20 million by 1980. Under FCC regulations, local governments
are responsible for awarding cable franchise privileges, while
cable operators themselves have the obligation of alloting time
to community groups. But a common complaint, access advocates say, is that many cable owners who hold an unfavorable
view of public access rights tend to give little or no assistance to
local users. It is further argued that operators who charge exor-
bitant rental fees for playback and studio facilities are not
meeting the FCC goal of providing low-cost community
television.

Current federal guidelines permit individual cable systems to
carry up to three "distant signal" stations. However, the recent
development of so-called "super signal" stations that combine
cable television and domestic communications satellites may
necessitate a reassessment of FCC policy. Satellites enable a
local broadcast outlet to become, in effect, a national station by
beaming its signal far greater distances than do conventional
broadcast towers. The use of such techniques has been a source
of concern to proponents of community access who fear "super
signal" cable broadcasts may preclude community-centered
programing. One "super signal" station, WTCG in Atlanta, is
already in operation. Plans are under way for similar stations in
Chicago, San Francisco and Los Angeles.

Carter's Proposals for Public Broadcasting

The Carter administration has underscored its determination
to expand community participation in public broadcasting. In
October it sent recommendations to Congress that are intended
to increase the level of federal subsidy for public radio and
television and to encourage more local programing. The White
House recommendations, written into the proposed Public
Broadcasting Financing Act of 1978, address such problems as
public accountability by individual stations, editorializing and
minority ownership.

The bill, now before the House Subcommittee on Communications, awaiting action in 1978, proposes raising the
funding authorization for public broadcasting from the present

---

[32] David Hoke, "Cable Access: Myth or Reality?" *Access,* November 1977, pp. 1-4. *Access*
is a monthly publication of the National Citizens Committee for Broadcasting.

level of $121-million in fiscal year 1978 to $200-million by 1981. In addition, the amount that stations must raise themselves in order to receive federal money would be lowered slightly. The current ratio is 250 to 100; 225 to 100 is the proposed ratio. Some media reformers have wondered if that ratio will be adequate, but a spokesman for the White House Office of Telecommunications Policy said the figure is not final and could be revised if circumstances warrant. The Carter legislation would also require public broadcast stations to open their meetings and their financial records to public scrutiny. The bill further proposes:

1. Earmarking 25 per cent of the money appropriated to the federal Corporation for Public Broadcasting to be used for program development, including local access programing.

2. Setting aside $30-million annually in grants to aid women and minorities who want to start public stations.

3. Lifting the current ban on editorializing from all stations not licensed to local or state governments. Under the terms of the bill, the ban would still apply, for example, to stations operated by community or state-supported colleges.

The prohibition against editorializing has been in effect since 1967 when Congress established the CPB.[33] But media reform groups as well as Carter administration officials now believe it should be removed so as to allow stations to air editorial comment on issues of public importance. "We cannot see why simply because a station bases its revenues on the sale of commercial products...it has a greater right or takes a greater risk in editorializing than one whose funds are a mixture of individual, foundation and corporate donations, and federal funds," said Frank Lloyd of the Office of Telecommunications.[34]

Media reform groups generally view the new proposals as a boost for public broadcasting. "What's most heartwarming about the Carter action," said Nicholas Johnson, chairman of the National Citizens Committee for Broadcasting, "is that it demonstrates that [the President] has taken the time and interest to grasp the potential and purpose and needs of this alternative broadcast system. It is the first time in 10 years, since President Johnson proposed the Corporation for Public Broadcasting, we could say that about a President...."[35] Yet while the government's change in attitude may be significant, it addresses only a part of the problem of public access to the media. The public demand is for a greater role in shaping broadcast and newspaper policies and practices.

---

[33] See "Financing of Educational Television," *E.R.R.*, 1967 Vol. I, pp. 161-180, and "Public Broadcasting in Britain and America," 1972 Vol. II, pp. 805-824.

[34] Testimony at hearings before the House Subcommittee on Communications, Oct. 19, 1977.

[35] Nicholas Johnson, "Carter Looks at Public Broadcasting," *Access,* November 1977, p. 8. Johnson served as chairman of the FCC from 1966 to 1973.

Selected Bibliography

Books

Barnouw, Erik, *Tube of Plenty: The Evolution of American Television,* Oxford, 1975.

Lazarus, Simon, *The Genteel Populists,* Holt, Rinehart and Winston, 1974.

Paletz, Donald L., Roberta E. Pearson and Donald L. Willis, *Politics in Public Service Advertising on Television,* Praeger, 1977.

Price, Monroe and John Wicklein, *Cable Television: A Guide for Citizen Action,* United Church, 1972.

Schorr, Daniel, *Clearing The Air,* Houghton Mifflin, 1977.

Schwartz, Barry N., ed., *Human Connection in the New Media,* Prentice Hall, 1973.

Smith, Ralph Lee, *The Wired Nation: Cable TV the Electronic Communications Highway,* Harper & Row, 1970.

Winn, Marie, *The Plug-In Drug: Television, Children and the Family,* Viking, 1977.

Articles

"America's Press: Too Much Power for Too Few?" *U.S. News & World Report,* Aug. 15, 1977.

Bagdikian, Ben H., "Woodstein U.: Notes on the Mass Production and Questionable Education of Journalists," *The Atlantic,* March 1977.

——"First Amendment Revisionism," *Columbia Journalism Review,* May-June 1974.

Broadcasting, selected issues.

Columbia Journalism Review, selected issues.

Epstein, Edward J., "Journalism and Truth," *Commentary,* April 1974.

Hamilton, John Maxwell, "Ombudsmen for the Press," *The Nation,* March 16, 1974.

"In-House Press Critics: A Selection of Recent Work by Newspaper Ombudsmen," *Columbia Journalism Review,* July-August 1977.

Mallette, M. F., "Should These News Pictures Have Been Printed?" *Popular Photography,* March 1976.

Mencher, Melvin, "The Arizona Project: An Appraisal," *Columbia Journalism Review,* November-December 1977.

[MORE], selected issues.

Powers, Thomas, "Right-to-Reply Laws," *Commonweal,* May 17, 1974,

Reports and Studies

Davis, Pamela, ed., "Citizens Media Directory," National Citizens Committee for Broadcasting, April 1977.

Editorial Research Reports, "Access to the Media," 1974 Vol. I, p. 447; "News Media Ownership," 1977 Vol. I, p. 183; "First Amendment and Mass Media," 1970 Vol. I, p. 41.

National Cable Television Association, "Guidelines for Access," August 1972.

U.S. Commission on Civil Rights, "Window Dressing on the Set: Women and Minorities in Television," August 1977.

INDEX

A

ABC. See American Broadcasting Co.
Accuracy in Media (AIM) - 163-164, 169
Action for Children's Television (ACT) - 167-169
Advertising, television
Child audiences - 167-168
Cigarettes - 175
Ethnic, sex stereotypes - 166-167
Aleman, José - 88
Alternate Media Center - 169
American Bar Association - 38, 131
American Broadcasting Co. (ABC)
Major network status - 3 (note)
Outlook - 16-19
Program violence ratings - 167
American Cancer Society - 175
American Civil Liberties Union - 131, 157
American College of Chest Physicians - 67
American College of Radiology - 67
American Demographics - 110, 119
American Newspaper Publishers Association (ANPA) - 23, 38, 175-177
American Society of Newspaper Editors - 43, 168
American Statistical Association - 112
Andrews, Dean A. Jr. - 94
Aspen Institute Program on Communications and Society - 169
Assassinations
Bibliography - 100
Conspiracy theories, psychological basis - 98-99
House Assassinations Committee - 83-88, 95, 97-98
Kennedy, John F.
Description of events - 88-90
Mafia role theory - 87-88
Oswald motive speculation - 86-87
Reopened case - 83-88, 95
Senate Intelligence Committee report - 94-95
Shaw conspiracy story - 93-94
Warren Commission report - 33, 83, 85-87, 90-95, 98
Kennedy, Robert F. - 96
King, Martin Luther Jr. - 84, 95-98
Presidents, total attempts - 99
Press, TV, recordings role - 84-87, 89, 93 (box), 94
Association of American Publishers - 44
Atomic energy. See Nuclear energy.
Atomic Energy Act of 1946 - 50-52
Atomic Energy Act of 1954 - 43, 48, 49, 54-55
Audio recordings
Assassinations investigations - 84-86
Legality, off-the-air recording - 12

B

Barabba, Vincent P. - 108
Bayh, Birch (D Ind.) - 38, 124, 136
Bell, Griffin B. - 124, 136
Black, Hugo L. - 34, 59
Blackmun, Harry A.
Gannett case - 26, 39
Herbert v. Lando - 27
Newsman's privilege - 36
Pentagon Papers case - 44
Supreme Court outlook - 38-39
Blakey, G. Robert - 95
Branzburg v. Hayes - 36
Brennan, William J. Jr.
Free press comments - 23, 31-32, 39
Gannett case - 26
Herbert v. Lando - 27
Newsman's privilege - 36
Newsroom searches - 28
Supreme Court outlook - 38
Wolston case - 27
Brooks, Jack (D Texas) - 135, 147
Bross, Irwin - 77, 78
Brown, Harold - 48
Burger, Warren E.
Burger Court on free press - 33-36
Free press comments - 24
Gannett case - 25, 39
Herbert v. Lando - 27
Newsman's privilege - 36
Newsroom searches - 28-29
Pentagon Papers - 44
Supreme Court outlook - 38
Business secrets protection - 138-139

C

Cable television
Background, development - 5-8, 145
Channel availability - 3, 154
Competition with network television - 3-4, 17-18
Definition - 5
Franchising competition (box) - 6
Information role - 154-155, 157
Pay-cable - 5-7, 17-18
Regulation - 4-5, 157, 177-178
Satellite transmissions - 6-9, 178
Superstations - 5, 8-9, 178
Cable Television Information Center - 169
Carter, President Jimmy
Atomic secrecy - 56-58
Breeder reactors - 70
Freedom of information - 124
Intelligence surveillance - 136-137
Newsroom search bill - 38
Privacy legislation - 127-128
Public broadcasting - 178-179
Radiation Inter-Agency Task Force - 75

O

P

Q

R

DATE DUE

OCT 4 '82			
GAYLORD			PRINTED IN U.S.A.